THE 17 ESSENTIAL
QUALITIES OF A
TEAM PLAYER

*Becoming the Kind of
Person Every Team Wants*

JOHN C. MAXWELL

THE 17 ESSENTIAL QUALITIES OF A TEAM PLAYER

Becoming the Kind of

Person Every Team Wants

Publishers Since 1798

THOMAS NELSON PUBLISHERS®
Nashville

A Division of Thomas Nelson, Inc.
www.ThomasNelson.com

Published in Nashville, Tennessee, by Thomas Nelson, Inc.

Unless otherwise noted, Scripture quotations are from the NEW
AMERICAN STANDARD BIBLE ®, © Copyright The Lockman
Foundation 1960, 1962, 1963, 1968, 1971, 1972, 1973, 1975, 1977.
Used by permission.

Library of Congress Cataloging-in-Publication Data

Maxwell, John C., 1947–
    The 17 essential qualities of a team player : becoming the kind of
person every team wants / John C. Maxwell.
      p. cm.
    Includes bibliographical references.
    ISBN 0-7852-7435-9
    1. Teams in the workplace—Psychological aspects. I. Title:
Seventeen essential qualities of a team player. II. Title.

HD66 .M374 2002
658.4'036—dc21   2001054676

Printed in the United States of America

02 03 04 05 06 BVG 5 4 3 2 1

This book is dedicated to the people on every team of which I've had the privilege of being a part.

To enhance and complete your learning experience,
we invite you to visit our companion Web site at
www.QualitiesOfATeamPlayer.com.
Here's how to use it and this book:

READ   *The 17 Essential Qualities of a Team Player.*

APPLY   what you learn by following the suggestions in
the "Bringing It Home" section in each chapter.

LOG ON   at www.QualitiesOfATeamPlayer.com to take the
free interactive assessment developed by The
INJOY Group. It will help you gauge your
strengths and weaknesses when it comes to the
qualities of a team player. There you will also find
recommendations for how you can further your
personal and professional development.

We hope you enjoy the book and the Web site, and we trust that
you will embrace the qualities of a team player to become the
kind of person every team wants.

Thomas Nelson Publishers and The INJOY Group

CONTENTS

ACKNOWLEDGMENTS

I'd like to say thank you to the people who helped me with this book. Every one of them is a true team player:

Linda Eggers, my administrative assistant
Kathie Wheat, my research assistant
Stephanie Wetzel, my proofreader
Charlie Wetzel, my writer

INTRODUCTION

You cannot build a great team without great players. That is a fact. As the saying goes, "You can lose with good players, but you cannot win without them." So how are you going to get good players? For that matter, how are you going to become a better player? When it comes to having good people on a team, you really have only two choices: train them or trade for them. You grow the players you already have into champions, or you go out and recruit championship-caliber people and bring them onto the team. This book can help you do either.

Developing a better team always begins with you. To improve the team, improve the individuals on the team. You can become a better team member by embracing the qualities outlined in the following pages. My recommendation is that you work your way through this book slowly. Read a chapter. Digest it. Use the "Bringing It Home" section to help you improve your grasp of each quality. If you want to assess yourself related to a particular quality, go to the Web site, *www.QualitiesOfATeamPlayer.com*.

By embracing the process, you can become the kind of person every team wants.

Improving yourself will add value to your team. But if you have a leadership role on your team, it's especially vital. Why? Because you can effectively teach only what you consistently model. It takes one to know one, show one, and grow one.

Once you model the behavior you expect from your teammates, begin using *The 17 Essential Qualities of a Team Player* as a training manual. You can use it to help your players become better team contributors—regardless of their level of talent. And if you desire to recruit new players from outside the team, turn to the book as a guide for finding the kinds of players who will put the team first. You can be sure that anyone who displays all seventeen qualities will be a team player.

God-given ability may be out of our control, but the ability to work as a team isn't. All people can choose to become better teammates. All they need to do is to embody the qualities of a team player. Do that yourself, help your teammates do the same, and the whole team will excel.

1

A D A P T A B L E

I F   Y O U   W O N ' T   C H A N G E   F O R   T H E   T E A M ,
T H E   T E A M   M A Y   C H A N G E   Y O U

Inflexibility is one of the worst human failings.
You can learn to check impetuosity, overcome fear with
confidence, and laziness with discipline.
But for rigidity of mind there is no antidote.
It carries the seeds of its own destruction.

—Anonymous

Blessed are the flexible,
for they shall not be bent out of shape.

—Michael McGriff

A BEBOP MIND

His friends call him Q. He has become a legend in the entertainment industry. He has worked with the best in the business, starting in the bebop era: Duke Ellington, Count Basie, Lionel Hampton, Frank Sinatra, Ella Fitzgerald, Sarah Vaughan, Ray Charles, Miles Davis, and the list goes on. He produced the best-selling music single of all time: "We Are the World." He produced the best-selling album of all time: Michael Jackson's *Thriller*. He has been nominated for more Grammy Awards than any other person, and as of today, he has won a total of twenty-seven. The person I'm talking about is Quincy Jones.

Quincy Jones was born in 1933 in Chicago and spent his first decade in one of the city's roughest neighborhoods. By his own admission, Jones says that he and his brother got into a lot of trouble in those early days. Then his family moved to Bremerton, Washington.

Soon afterward Jones discovered his love for music. At age eleven, he decided that he wanted to play an instrument. So he started with percussion. Even back then he showed signs of a quality that would mark him as a professional—his adaptability. He began staying after school and trying out a variety of other instruments. He tried the clarinet and violin, but ultimately he was attracted to brass. So he tried out all the brass instruments: baritone, French horn, sousaphone, and trombone. Finally he landed on the trumpet, and he excelled.

By age fourteen, he had his first paying job as a musician. As a teenager, he became friends with Ray Charles, who is just a few years older than he. Jones began to compose music and to learn how to do arrangements. And when the best bands and singers came through Seattle, he either went to hear them play or played with them. At age eighteen, he was on the road touring with Lionel Hampton.

Jones has always displayed a strong hunger to learn—which he calls an "obsessive curiosity"—and an amazing adaptability. Through the years, he has easily transitioned from musician to arranger to band leader. In the 1950s, he worked with many of the greatest jazz performers. In 1957, when he thought he could use more education, he moved to Paris and studied under Nadia Boulanger, who had tutored Aaron Copland and Leonard Bernstein.

At that time, Jones took a position with Mercury Records to make ends meet. That's where he learned the business side of the music industry. He was so good at it that in 1964 the company made him a vice president. (He was the first African-American to hold an executive position at a major record company.) It was also in the sixties that Jones decided to tackle a new challenge: scoring movies. He has gone on to write music for more than thirty movies and numerous television programs.

Throughout his career, Jones has worked with the best singers and musicians in the world. Because he spent so much time in the jazz community, when he worked with Michael Jackson in 1982, some of his colleagues accused him of selling out. Jones thought that was ridiculous, as he explained:

When I was twelve to thirteen years old, we played every-thing—strip music, rhythm and blues. We played pop music, schottisches [similar to polkas], and Sousa . . . We played every club in town—black, white, tennis clubs. So, I've always had a range of styles to draw from. Working with Michael Jackson or Frank Sinatra has never been a stretch. Bebop was one thing I was deeply involved with musically, and bebop does affect your thinking. It takes you away from being rigid and helps you always keep your mind wide open.[1]

His flexibility and creativity have served Jones well. They have not only enabled him to work with all kinds of musicians—from Latin to pop and from jazz to rap—but they have also made it possible for him to bring the best out of any person he works with. He adapts to the person and the situation to create a win for everyone. "Everyone has a different way of relating to people," observed Jones. "I take everybody one-on-one, and I'm happy I do because I've had some great relationships that transcend show business."[2]

Jones himself has transcended professionally. He has used his adaptability to branch out into other industries. He broke into filmmaking when he coproduced *The Color Purple.* Then he took on television, producing several hit shows including *The Fresh Prince of Bel-Air.* Jones and several partners launched Qwest Broadcasting, and he is also the founder and chairman of *Vibe* magazine.

To Jones, being able to adjust or stretch himself is not a big thing; it's just who he is. Currently he's working on writing a Broadway show based on the life of Sammy Davis Jr. He says it makes him feel like he's fifteen years old. Jones has never been afraid of a new idea, a new team, a new industry. Challenges have been no problem to him because he is so incredibly adaptable.

F L E S H I N G   I T   O U T

Teamwork and personal rigidity just don't mix. If you want to work well with others and be a good team player, you have to be willing to adapt yourself to your team. Harvard Business School professor Rosabeth Moss Kanter observed, "The individuals who will succeed and flourish will also be masters of change: adept at reorienting their own and others' activities in untried directions to bring about higher levels of achievement."

> **Teamwork and personal rigidity just don't mix.**

Team players who exhibit adaptability have certain characteristics. Adaptable people are . . .

1. Teachable

Diana Nyad said, "I am willing to put myself through anything; temporary pain or discomfort means nothing to me as long as I can see that the experience will take me to a new level. I am interested in the unknown, and the only path to the unknown is through breaking barriers." Adaptable people always place a high priority on breaking new ground. They are highly teachable.

Look at Quincy Jones and you see someone who is always learning. His belief is that if a person works hard and becomes highly skilled in one area, he can transfer that ability to new endeavors. That approach can work for anyone who's teachable. On the other hand, unteachable people have a difficult time with change, and as a result they never adapt well.

2. Emotionally Secure

Another characteristic of adaptable people is security. People who are not emotionally secure see almost everything as a challenge or a threat. They meet with rigidity or suspicion the addition of another talented person to the team, an alteration in their position or title, or a change in the way things are done. But secure people aren't made nervous by change itself. They evaluate a new situation or a change in their responsibilities based on its merit.

> A person's age can be determined by the degree of pain he experiences when he comes in contact with a new idea.
>
> —QUINCY JONES

3. Creative

Creativity is another quality you find in adaptable people. When difficult times come, they find a way. Quincy Jones remarked,

> There's an expression that says a person's age can be determined by the degree of pain he experiences when he comes

in contact with a new idea. Somebody might say, "Let's try it this new way." You can actually see the pain. These people will grab their heads. It physically hurts to think of doing something different. The ones who don't react with fear are the really creative people. "Let's try it," they'll say. "Let's go there even if we blow it."[3]

Creativity fosters adaptability.

4. Service Minded

People who are focused on themselves are less likely to make changes for the team than people focused on serving others. Educator and college president Horace Mann stated, "Doing nothing for others is the undoing of one's self." If your goal is to serve the team, adapting to accomplish that goal isn't difficult.

R EFLECTING on I T

How are you when it comes to adaptability? If improving the team requires you to change the way you do things, how do you react? Are you supportive, or would you rather do things the way they've "always been done before"? If someone with greater talent in your current area joins the team, would you be willing to take on a different role? Or if a key player in another area is having a problem, are you willing to change positions to help out? The first key to being a team player is being willing to adapt yourself to the team— not an expectation that the team will adapt to you!

BRINGING IT HOME

To become more adaptable . . .

- *Get into the habit of learning.* For many years I carried a three-by-five card in my pocket. Every day when I learned something new, I'd write it down on the card. By the end of the day, I'd try to share the idea with a friend or colleague and then file the idea for future use. It got me in the habit of *looking* for things to learn. Try it for a week and see what happens.

- *Reevaluate your role.* Spend some time looking at your current role on your team. Then try to discover whether there is another role you could fulfill as well or better than you do your current one. That process may prompt you to make a transition, but even if it doesn't, the mental exercise will increase your flexibility.

- *Think outside the lines.* Let's face it: many people aren't adaptable because they get into negative ruts. If you tend to be prone to ruts, then write down this phrase and keep it where you can see it every day: "Not why it *can't* be done but how it *can* be done." Look for unconventional solutions every time you meet a challenge. You'll be surprised by how creative you can become if you continually strive to do so.

8

One of the greatest generals in military history was Napoleon Bonaparte. Made a full general at age twenty-six, he utilized shrewd strategy, bold cunning, and lightning speed to his advantage to win many victories. The Duke of Wellington, one of the general's most formidable enemies, said, "I consider Napoleon's presence in the field to equal forty thousand men in the balance."

"I will tell you the mistake you are always making," Napoleon said, addressing an opponent he had defeated. "You draw up your plans the day before battle, when you do not yet know your adversary's movements." Napoleon recognized in his losing opponent a weakness that he himself did not have: lack of adaptability. If you are willing to change and adapt for the sake of your team, you always have a chance to win.

COMPANION **ONLINE** RESOURCE

Learn more about yourself and this quality of a team player by taking the FREE assessment at **QualitiesOfATeamPlayer.com**.

2

COLLABORATIVE

WORKING TOGETHER PRECEDES WINNING TOGETHER

All your strength is in union,
all your danger is in discord.

—*Henry Wadsworth Longfellow*

Collaboration is multiplication.

—*John C. Maxwell*

UNDERGROUND MOVEMENT

They called it the Great Escape. It wasn't great because it had never been done before. Prisoners of war had previously escaped from enemy camps. It wasn't called great because of the outcome: the results were terrible for most of the escapees. It was great because the scale of it made the task seem impossible!

Stalag Luft III, a Nazi prisoner-of-war camp one hundred miles southeast of Berlin, was a huge compound that once held as many as 10,000 Allied POWs. Within that camp in 1944 was a core group of prisoners determined to escape. In fact, their goal was to facilitate the escape of no fewer than 250 men in one night, something that would require the utmost cooperation among the prisoners. An escape so daunting had never been tried before.

Getting men out of a German prison camp was a very complex task. Of course there was the challenge of digging and hiding the tunnels that would provide the means of escape. Together, prisoners engineered the tunnels, dug them, shored them up with wooden slats taken from prisoners' beds, and disposed of the dirt in amazingly creative ways. They pumped air into the tunnels with homemade bellows. They created tracks and trolleys used by men to move through the tunnels. They even wired the narrow passages with electric lights. The list of supplies needed for the job was unbelievable: 4,000 bed slats, 1,370 battens, 1,699 blankets, 52 long tables, 1,219 knives, 30 shovels, 600 feet of rope, 1,000 feet of electric wire, and more.[1] It took an army of prisoners just to find and steal all the materials for the tunnels.

However difficult building the tunnels was, creating the means of escape was only part of the whole project. Every man who would attempt escape needed a host of supplies and equipment: civilian clothes, German papers and identity cards, maps, homemade compasses, emergency rations, and other items. Several prisoners continually scrounged for anything that might aid the team. Others worked systematically and relentlessly at bribing and then blackmailing the guards.

Each person had a job. There were tailors, blacksmiths, pickpockets, and forgers who worked secretly month after month. The prisoners even developed teams of men who specialized in distraction and camouflage, keeping the German soldiers off guard.

Perhaps the most challenging job was that of "security." Since the Germans employed many guards who specialized in escape detection—called ferrets by the prisoners—the security team kept a log of every movement of every guard who came through the compound. And they used an elaborate, yet inconspicuous, set of signals to warn other security men, lookouts, and working team members when a guard posed a threat to their efforts.

On the night of March 24, 1944, after more than a year of work, 220 men prepared to creep through the tunnel and into the woods outside the prison camp. The plan was to send out one man per minute until all had made their escape. German-speaking prisoners would board trains and pose as foreign workers. The rest would lie low during the day and travel at night, hoping to avoid German patrols.

When the first prisoner popped up out of the tunnel, though, he discovered that its exit was short of the woods. Rather than get out a man per minute, they were barely able to get out a dozen per hour. In all, eighty-six men escaped before the tunnel was discovered. It created chaos for the Nazis, who ordered a national alert to deal with it. Eighty-three of the prisoners were captured, and forty-one of them were executed by order of Adolf Hitler. Only three made it to freedom.

John Sturges, the man who directed the 1963 movie *The Great Escape* based on the real event, said of the prisoners' effort, "It demanded the concentrated devotion and vigilance of more than 600 men—every single one of them, every minute, every hour, every day and every night for more than a year. Never has the human capacity been stretched to such incredible lengths or shown with as much determination and courage."[2]

FLESHING IT OUT

Great challenges require great teamwork, and the quality most needed among teammates amid the pressure of a difficult challenge is collaboration. Notice that I didn't say "cooperation" because collaboration is more than that. Cooperation is working together agreeably. Collaboration is working together aggressively. Collaborative teammates do more than just work with one another. Each person brings something to the table that adds value to the relationship and synergy to the team. The sum of truly collaborative teamwork is always greater than its parts.

Becoming a collaborative team player requires a change in focus in four areas:

1. Perception: See Teammates as Collaborators, Not Competitors

Look at any team, and you can see the potential for competition. Siblings fight for their parents' attention. Coworkers compete for raises and promotions. Ballplayers go head-to-head to see who will be the starter and who will sit on the bench. Because all people have hopes, goals, and dreams, they want to achieve. But to collaborative team members, completing one another is more important than competing with one another. They perceive themselves as a unit working together, and they never allow competition between teammates to get to the point where it hurts the team.

> To collaborative team members, completing one another is more important than competing with one another.

2. Attitude: Be Supportive, Not Suspicious, of Teammates

Some people are so preoccupied with looking out for their own interests that they are naturally suspicious of just about everyone, including their teammates. But adopting the mind-set where you complete rather than compete with teammates is possible only if you suspend your suspicions and become a supportive team player.

It's a matter of attitude. That means assuming that other people's motives are good unless proven otherwise. If you trust people, you will treat them better. And if you treat them better, you and they will be more likely to create collaborative relationships.

3. Focus: Concentrate on the Team, Not on Yourself

As a person on a team, you will usually ask one of two questions when anything happens: "What's in it for me?" or "What does this do for the team?" Where you focus your attention says a lot about whether you compete with others or complete them. Author Cavett Roberts points out, "True progress in any field is a relay race and not a single event." If you focus on the team and not just yourself, you will be able to pass the baton when necessary instead of trying to complete the race by yourself.

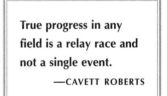

True progress in any field is a relay race and not a single event.

—CAVETT ROBERTS

4. Results: Create Victories Through Multiplication

When you work together with your teammates, you can do remarkable things. If you work alone, you leave a lot of victories on the table. Collaboration has a multiplying effect on everything you do because it releases and harnesses not only your skills but also those of everyone on the team.

R E F L E C T I N G   O N   I T

Are you a collaborative person? You may not be working *against* the team, but that doesn't necessarily mean you're working *for* it. Do you bring cooperation and added value to your teammates—even to the people you don't enjoy being with? Do you help to multiply the efforts of others? Or does the team become slower and less effective when you're involved? If you're not sure, talk to your teammates.

B R I N G I N G   I T   H O M E

To become a collaborative team player . . .

- *Think win-win-win.* King Solomon of ancient Israel observed, "Iron sharpens iron, so one man sharpens another."[3] Usually when you collaborate with others, you win, they win, and the team wins. Find someone on the team with a similar role whom you have previously seen as a competitor. Figure out ways you can share information and work together to benefit both you and the team.

- *Complement others.* Another way to collaborate is to get together with someone who has strengths in your area of weakness and vice versa. Seek out others on the team with complementary gifts and work together.

- *Take yourself out of the picture.* Get in the habit of asking what's best for the team. For example, the next time you are at a problem-solving meeting and everyone is contributing ideas, instead of promoting yourself, ask yourself how the team would do if you were not

> **Usually when you collaborate with others, you win, they win, and the team wins.**

involved in the solution. If it would do better, then propose ideas that promote and involve people other than yourself.

D A I L Y   T A K E - A W A Y

Some boys were hiking in the woods one day when they came across part of an old abandoned railroad track stretching off through the trees. One of the boys jumped up onto a rail and tried walking on it. After a few steps, he lost his balance. Another boy soon tried the same thing, and he also fell. The others laughed.

"I bet you can't do it either," he barked at the others. One by one, the boys tried it, but they all failed. Even the best athlete of the bunch couldn't go more than a dozen steps without stumbling.

Then two of the boys began whispering to each other, and one of them challenged the others: "I can walk on the rail all the way to the end, and so can he." He pointed to his buddy.

"No, you can't," said one of the other boys who had tried and failed.

"Bet you a candy bar each we can!" he answered, and the other boys accepted.

Then each of the two boys who had issued the challenge hopped up onto a rail, reached out an arm, locked hands with the other, and carefully walked the whole distance.

As individuals, they could not meet the challenge. But working together, they easily won. The power of collaboration is multiplication.

COMPANION **ONLINE** RESOURCE

Learn more about yourself and this quality of a team player by taking the FREE assessment at **QualitiesOfATeamPlayer.com**.

3

COMMITTED

THERE ARE NO HALFHEARTED CHAMPIONS

The moment one definitely commits oneself,
then Providence moves too. All sorts of things occur
to help one that would never otherwise have occurred.
A whole stream of events issue from the decision,
raising in one's favor all manner of unforeseen incidents
and meetings and material assistance which no man
could have dreamed would come his way.

—William H. Murray

Ordinary people with commitment
can make an extraordinary impact on their world.

—John C. Maxwell

TAKING ONE FOR THE TEAM

In 1939, a twenty-five-year-old man from New York City named Jonas Salk completed his training at NYU Medical School. As a boy, he had dreamed of becoming a lawyer, but somewhere between his graduation from high school and his entrance into college, his interest shifted from the laws of the land to the laws of nature. He decided that he wanted to be a doctor. Perhaps he made the switch because his mother had discouraged his pursuit of law. "My mother didn't think I would make a very good lawyer," he remarked years later, "probably because I could never win an argument with her."[1] His working-class immigrant parents were proud when he graduated with his medical degree because he was the first person in his family to have received an education.

Though he chose to become a doctor, Salk's real passion was research. He was intrigued by contradictory scientific claims by two professors, which prompted him to begin studying immunology, including influenza research. And during his second year of medical school, when he got the chance to spend a year doing research and teaching, he took it. "At the end of that year," he recalled, "I was told I could, if I wished, switch and get a Ph.D. in biochemistry but my preference was to stay with medicine. I believe that this is all linked to my original ambition, or desire, which was to be of some help to humankind, so to speak, in a larger sense than just on a one-to-one basis."[2]

In 1947, Salk became the head of the Virus Research Lab at

the University of Pittsburgh. It was there that he began investigating the polio virus. In those days, polio was a horrible, disabling disease that claimed the lives of thousands of people every year, with children being the most frequent victims. The New York polio epidemic of the summer of 1916 left 27,000 people paralyzed and another 9,000 people dead. After that year, epidemics became common, and every summer hordes of people escaped large cities to try to protect their children.

In the first half of the twentieth century, viral research was still in its infancy. But in 1948, a team of scientists at Harvard University discovered how to produce large quantities of viruses in laboratories, and that made more extensive research possible. Salk capitalized on those scientists' findings and others' groundbreaking work and began developing a polio vaccine.

After more than four years of continuous work, Salk and his team at the University of Pittsburgh developed a vaccine in 1952. They did some safe preliminary testing with it on people who had previously contracted polio and survived. But the true test would be injecting the vaccine, which contained inactive polio cells, into people who had never had polio.

Salk had shown his dedication to helping people through years of study, preparation, and research. However, it's one thing to believe in something you're doing, and another to be totally committed to it. In the summer of 1952, Jonas Salk inoculated healthy volunteers with his vaccine. Included in that group were himself, his wife, and their three sons. He was committed!

Salk's commitment paid off. The trials of the vaccine were

successful, and in 1955, he and his former mentor, Dr. Thomas Francis, arranged to inoculate 4 million children. In 1955, there were 28,985 cases of polio reported in the United States. In 1956, that number was cut in half. In 1957, there were only 5,894. Today, thanks to the work of Jonas Salk and subsequent efforts by other scientists such as Albert Sabin, cases of polio in the U.S. are virtually nonexistent.

Jonas Salk dedicated eight years of his life to defeating polio. But his real desire was to help people, which he further demonstrated by never patenting the vaccine he created. In that way, it could be used to help people around the globe. You could say that the team he was most committed to was mankind.

FLESHING IT OUT

Many people tend to associate commitment with their emotions. If they feel the right way, then they can follow through on their commitments. But true commitment doesn't work that way. It's not an emotion; it's a character quality that enables us to reach our goals. Human emotions go up and down all the time, but commitment has to be rock solid. If you want a solid team—whether it's a business, ball club, marriage, or volunteer organization—you must have team players who are solidly committed to the team.

There are some things every team player needs to know about being committed:

1. Commitment Usually Is Discovered in the Midst of Adversity

People don't really know whether they are committed to something until they face adversity. Struggles strengthen a person's resolve. Adversity fosters commitment, and commitment fosters hard work. And the more you work at something, the less likely you are to give up on it. As NFL Hall of Fame coach Vince Lombardi said, "The harder you work, the harder it is to surrender." Committed people don't surrender easily.

> **The harder you work, the harder it is to surrender.**
>
> —VINCE LOMBARDI

2. Commitment Does Not Depend on Gifts or Abilities

Sometimes when we know of talented people who are highly successful, we may be tempted to think that commitment is easier for them because of their talent. It seems as if it might be easier for first-rate athletes to practice or skilled artists to refine their craft or natural businesspeople to work at their businesses. But that isn't true. Commitment and talent are unconnected—unless you connect them.

Haven't you known highly talented people who have squandered their potential because they wouldn't *do* anything? And don't you know people less talented than you who are more successful? That is often due, in part, to commitment. Author Basil Walsh said, "We don't need more strength or more ability or greater opportunity. What we need to use is what we have." If we will commit ourselves to using what talent we have, then we will find that we have more talent—and more to offer our team— as the result of our commitment.

3. Commitment Comes as the Result of Choice, Not Conditions

When it comes right down to it, commitment is always a matter of choice. In *Choices,* Frederic F. Flach writes,

> Most people look back over the years and identify a time and place at which their lives changed significantly. Whether by accident or design, these are the moments when, because of a readiness within us and a collaboration with events occurring around us, we are forced to seriously reappraise ourselves and the conditions under which we live and to make certain choices that will affect the rest of our lives.[3]

Far too many people think that conditions determine choices. More often, choices determine conditions. When you choose commitment, you give yourself a chance for success.

4. Commitment Lasts When It's Based on Values

It's one thing to make a commitment in a moment. It's another to stick with it. How do you remain committed? The answer lies in what you base your commitments on. Anytime you make choices based on solid life values, then you are in a better position to sustain your level of commitment because you don't have to continually reevaluate its importance. It's like settling the issue before it is tested. A commitment to something you believe in is a commitment that is easier to keep.

> **Anytime you make choices based on solid life values, then you are in a better position to sustain your level of commitment.**

R E F L E C T I N G   O N   I T

How important is commitment to you? Are you someone who values loyalty and follow-through? When things get tough, are you in the habit of standing firm? Or do you have a tendency to compromise or even quit? More specifically, how committed are you to your team? Is your support solid? Is your dedication undeniable? Or are you tentative in your level of commitment? If you find yourself reevaluating your intention to stay with the team whenever you and your teammates face adversity, then you may need to become more committed.

B R I N G I N G   I T   H O M E

To improve your level of commitment . . .

- *Tie your commitments to your values.* Because your values and your ability to fulfill your commitments are closely related, take some time to reflect on them. First, make a list of your personal and professional commitments. Then try to articulate your core values. (This will take some time, especially if you've never done it before, so don't rush it.) Once you have both lists, compare them. You will probably find that you have commitments unrelated to your values. Reevaluate them. You will also find that you have values that you are not living out. Commit yourself to them.

- *Take a risk.* Being committed involves risk. You may fail. Your teammates may let you down. You may discover that fulfilling your goals doesn't give you the results you desire. But take the risk of committing anyway. George Halas, former owner of the NFL Chicago Bears, asserted, "Nobody who ever gave his best regretted it."

- *Evaluate your teammates' commitment.* If you find it difficult to commit in particular relationships and you cannot find a reason for it in yourself, consider this: you cannot make a commitment to uncommitted people and expect to receive a commitment from them. Examine the relationship to see whether you are reluctant because the potential recipient is untrustworthy.

> Nobody who ever gave his best regretted it.
> —GEORGE HALAS

DAILY TAKE-AWAY

How do you define true commitment? Let me tell you how Hernán Cortés defined it. In 1519, under the sponsorship of Cuba's

Governor Velásquez, Cortés sailed from Cuba to the Mexican mainland with the goal of gaining riches for Spain and fame for himself. Though only thirty-four years old, the young Spanish captain had prepared his whole life for such a chance.

But the soldiers under his command were not as dedicated as he. After he landed, there was talk that the men might mutiny and return to Cuba with his ships. What was his solution? He burned the ships. How dedicated are you to your team? Are you totally committed, or do you have an "out," just in case things don't work out? If so, maybe you need to burn a ship or two. Remember, there is no such thing as a halfhearted champion.

COMPANION
ONLINE
RESOURCE

Learn more about yourself and this quality of a team player by taking the FREE assessment at **QualitiesOfATeamPlayer.com.**

C O M M U N I C A T I V E

A T E A M I S M A N Y V O I C E S
W I T H A S I N G L E H E A R T

If you have not a good degree of eloquence in speaking
and writing you will be nobody; but will have the daily
mortification of seeing people with not one-tenth part
of your merit or knowledge get the start of you.

—*Lord Chesterford*

Think like a wise man
but communicate in the language of the people.

—*William Butler Yeats*

THE TEAM THAT SAVED A TOWN

A few years ago, screenwriter Gregory Allen Howard moved from Los Angeles to Alexandria, Virginia. He was no stranger to the state, having spent some of his growing-up years in Norfolk, but he found that he especially liked Alexandria. It had the historical interest of having been George Washington's hometown, but the thing that really impressed Howard, an African-American, was that black and white people lived and worked closely together, unlike in many other parts of the South.

One day after he had settled in, Howard was at a barbershop and heard men talking about a local high school football team and how great it was. They went on and on about the players and their accomplishments. Finally Howard asked where the team would be playing their next game so that he could watch them. That's when he found out that the team the men loved was from 1971!

Howard couldn't believe it. After nearly three decades, that particular team was just as important to the people of the town as a team that was still playing. Howard got to thinking. Then he started researching. The more he found out, the more intrigued he became. He decided to write a screenplay about the true events surrounding that team, and that script was made into a movie called *Remember the Titans*.

If you've seen the movie, you probably remember that it was set at a time when many communities in the United States were in the process of dismantling segregation. In 1971, the town of Alexandria took tangible steps toward racial equality when it combined the populations of three high schools—two white and one black—into a new integrated school call T. C. Williams High School.

It was a difficult time, and people from both racial communities were tense over the forced interaction. The first groups to come together were the black and white high school football players who were on a team together for the first time. Adding to the tension was the fact that Herman Boone, a black coach, was selected to be the head coach of the Williams football team rather than Bill Yoast, a local white coach who was very popular in the community.

Boone did everything in his power to bring the players of that team together. He forced black and white players to ride on the buses together up to training camp. He also made them room together, but he was having a hard time getting them to come together as a team. The players kept separating themselves by race—all but one white player. In a pivotal moment in the movie, Coach Boone asks that white team member for some facts about some of his African-American teammates. The player easily answers the questions. That's when the coach tells all of the young men that until they all learn about every other player on the team, they can expect to endure grueling practices three times a day. It didn't occur easily, nor did it happen overnight, but the team started to come together.

Years later when asked in an interview what the keys were to getting the team to bond, Herman Boone said, "Winning did it. Winning solves everything . . . It's also about communication.

Talking to each other. We forced the kids to spend time with each other, [to] find out things about each other. Every player was required to spend time with teammates [who] were a different race."[1]

That action turned the Titans around. And the team did win. They won every game of their regular season, the play-offs, and the state championship. By the time they were finished, the Titans of 1971 were ranked the second best high school team in the nation. But more important than their wins on the field was their impact off it. In response to the Titans, the president of the United States, who lived less than ten miles away across the Potomac River, stated simply, "The team saved the city of Alexandria."[2]

Boone agreed. He remarked,

> The town decided to follow the team rather than those who wanted to tear the team and the town down. I believe the team did play a great role in keeping the city calm, focused, positive towards these young men who'd shown the city that you can get along if you just talk to each other. It was a powerful message that they passed on for generations, and it will be passed on for generations . . . At a time when the city was ready to burn itself to the ground, these kids stepped out and changed attitudes among themselves and their community.[3]

And that is why to this day the people of Alexandria still remember—and talk about—the Titans.

FLESHING IT OUT

To state it bluntly, you cannot have teamwork unless you have communicative players. Without communication, you don't have a team; you have a collection of individuals.

If you evaluate a good team, you will find that its players have some common characteristics. Communicative players . . .

1. Do Not Isolate Themselves from Others

The key problem Herman Boone had to overcome on his newly formed team was isolation. The players of one race isolated themselves from the players of the other. Anytime a player becomes isolated, it is a problem for the team. If entire sections of the team become isolated, that problem grows. The more teammates know about each other and about the team's goals and methods, the more they'll understand. The more they understand, the more they'll care. A player with passion as well as information and connection is a powerful asset to the team.

2. Make It Easy for Teammates to Communicate with Them

Most communication problems can be solved with proximity. That's why Herman Boone used it to get his team to gel. Putting players of different races on the same buses and forcing them to room with one another made communication more likely to happen. If you look at good

> **Most communication problems can be solved with proximity.**

leaders and impact players on a team, you will find that they not only stay connected with their teammates; they also make sure their teammates are able to make contact with them easily.

3. *Follow the Twenty-Four-Hour Rule*

When some people are faced with conflict or interpersonal difficulties, they avoid the person with whom they are having the problem. But time alone doesn't usually fix such situations. Without knowing both sides of the story, people tend to give the benefit of the doubt to themselves and to assign negative motives and actions to others. Without communication, the situation just festers.

That's why team members need to follow the twenty-four-hour rule. If you have any kind of difficulty or conflict with a teammate, don't let more than twenty-four hours go by without addressing it. In fact, the sooner you communicate, usually the better off you and your teammates will be.

4. *Give Attention to Potentially Difficult Relationships*

Relationships need attention to thrive. That is especially true of relationships between people who have potential for conflict. One of the most volatile relationships on the Titans' team was that between white linebacker Gerry Bertier and black defensive end Julius Campbell. The two started out hating each other, and they butted heads constantly. But through the course of the season, they became fast friends. When Bertier was paralyzed in an auto accident and lying in his hospital bed, the first person he asked for was Julius. Their relationship may have developed slowly, but it grew strong. What Aristotle said is true: "Friendship is a slow-ripening fruit."

5. Follow Up Important Communication in Writing

The more difficult communication becomes, the more important it is to work to keep it clear and simple. That often means putting communication in writing. It's not accidental that most marriages have vows, football teams have playbooks, and partnerships have contracts. When communication with your teammates is important, you'll find it's easier to keep everyone on the same page if you've written it down for everyone's benefit.

REFLECTING ON IT

How are you doing when it comes to communication? Are you well connected to all of your teammates? Have you neglected some people or excluded them from your circle of communication? Or have you isolated yourself from others for the sake of being more productive? (Recognize that you may accomplish more individual goals that way, but you may be hurting the team's productivity.) How about accessibility? Can members of your team get to you, or do you make it hard for them to follow the twenty-four-hour rule? Anytime you're on a team but not communicating with team members, the team suffers.

> **Open communication fosters trust.**

B R I N G I N G   I T   H O M E

To improve your communication . . .

- *Be candid.* Open communication fosters trust. Having hidden agendas, communicating to people via a third party, and sugarcoating bad news hurt team relationships. Think about a poor relationship you have with someone on your team. If you haven't been candid with that person, then determine to change your ways. Your goal should be to speak truthfully but kindly to your teammates.

- *Be quick.* If you tend to sit on things instead of saying them, force yourself to follow the twenty-four-hour rule. When you discover an issue with teammates, find the first reasonable opportunity to address it with them. And invite others to do the same with you.

- *Be inclusive.* Some people hoard information unless forced to divulge it. Don't take that approach. If you *can* include others, do. Certainly you need to be discreet with sensitive information, but remember this: people are *up* on things they're *in* on. Open communication increases trust, trust increases ownership, and ownership increases participation.

> **People are *up* on things they're *in* on.**

DAILY TAKE-AWAY

A story called "The Lion and the Three Bulls," written by the Greek fable writer Aesop, gives insight into how important it is for teammates to be communicative. Three bulls lived together for a long time in a pasture. Though they ate and lived side by side, they never spoke with one another. One day a lion came along and saw the bulls. The lion was very hungry, but he knew that he could never attack three bulls at once because together they would overpower him and kill him. So the lion approached the bulls one at a time. Since one bull never knew what the others were doing, they didn't realize that the lion was working to separate them. The lion, who was crafty, succeeded in dividing them, and with them successfully isolated, he attacked them individually. Thus he overcame all three of them and satisfied his hunger.

Aesop concluded the story by stating, "Union is strength." But there can be no union without good communication.

COMPANION **ONLINE** RESOURCE

Learn more about yourself and this quality of a team player by taking the FREE assessment at **QualitiesOfATeamPlayer.com**.

5

COMPETENT

IF YOU CAN'T, YOUR TEAM WON'T

The quality of a person's life is in direct
proportion to their commitment to excellence,
regardless of their chosen field of endeavor.

—*Vince Lombardi*

People forget how fast you did a job—
but they remember how well you did it.

—*Howard W. Newton*

WIZARD OF THE WOOD SHOP

When I was the senior pastor at Skyline Church in California, I became friends with a wonderful man in my congregation named Bob Taylor, who eventually became the vice chairman of my church board. Bob has always liked to build and tinker. When he was a kid and got something on Christmas morning, chances were that before the sun went down that night, he had taken apart his gift to see how it worked. And most of the time, he put it back together, and it still worked. He had a special knack for it.

Once as a kid, when his mom was on the telephone, he and his friends were jumping on the couch when they heard a loud crack. They had broken the frame of the couch, and it was resting on the floor! Before his mom completed her phone conversation, he had found the problem and then glued, clamped, and screwed together the broken wood to repair it. Good as new.

It was natural that when he got to junior high and then high school, he took every industrial arts class he could. "I had some great teachers," Bob recalls. "I had one who would open up the shop even on holiday weekends so that I could keep working on my projects."

One of Bob's other interests is music. When Bob was in high school, he decided he wanted a good twelve-string guitar. He had started playing when he was in third grade after a neighbor had given him an inexpensive guitar (which he subsequently sawed open to see how it was built). The only problem was that Bob didn't really have the money to go out and buy the instrument he wanted. *No problem*, he figured, *I'll just make one myself.* And he did—as an eleventh-grade wood shop project! In fact, while in high school, he made not one but three guitars and a banjo.

Lots of people pick up interesting hobbies in high school. Some individuals continue to pursue those hobbies. Others drop them as they grow older. But Bob did something really special with his. You see, if you play guitar, you've probably walked into a music store and seen a Taylor guitar. Yes, he's *that* Bob Taylor. He went from building guitars in his spare time as a teenager to cofounding his own company.

Bob's business partner of twenty-seven years, Kurt Listug, has the passion for marketing and building a business while Bob provides the passion and technical expertise for building guitars. Today Taylor Guitars constructs some of the finest acoustic guitars in the world, and the manufacturing plant does it at the pace of two hundred instruments a day.

What has enabled Bob to go from solitary luthier to employer of more than 450 people who occupy a 124,000-square-foot complex? The answer lies in his incredible competence and tireless dedication to excellence.

"I'm a 'tweak head,'" says Bob. "I'm continually trying to refine the process." That desire is focused on more than just the guitars themselves. True, Bob Taylor has introduced numerous innovations to guitar building. But Bob's real focus is on the manufacturing process and on the people who build the guitars.

> **Building the team is as important as producing the product.**
>
> **—BOB TAYLOR**

"Good guitars are really the by-product of good tools and a good facility," explains Bob. "And of course the people part is so important. Building the team is as important as producing the product. You have to let the people be a team. That means fostering an environment where people say what they really think. You can't be too dogmatic." That attitude has allowed the best ideas to rise to the top and get implemented.

"One of the things I've found with people is that they don't want to let the next person onto the team," observes Bob. "Once they get on the team, they want to keep it the way it is. They say they're doing it to protect the quality. But I tell them, 'Don't you think I have the same concern? If I were like you, *you* wouldn't be on the team.' To keep getting better, you have to let people come onto the team and let the quality of the product suffer for a while. It's a constant struggle to achieve."

It's easy to talk about letting the quality suffer in the short term when your competence is so high and your product is so good that even at its worst, it is better than most in your industry. But that willingness to risk and innovate keeps paying off with better guitars. Right now Bob and his team are working on their newest innovation in the area of acoustic guitar amplification. "We're about one year into the process of designing pick-ups [electronic devices that 'pick up' a guitar's sound]," says Bob, "and we've got about another year to go. It's the closest to pure invention we've ever come. We started from scratch with a blank sheet of paper and asked, 'What do we want?' Now we're creating it."

Bob continues, "You know, inspiration is easy. Implementation is the hard part." Implementation may not be easy,

> ... inspiration is easy. Implementation is the hard part.
>
> —BOB TAYLOR

but Bob continues to succeed because of his competence and dedication to following through.

Bob's daughter, Minét, sums up his ability by saying, "He has this amazing desire to always make things better. If there is a way to improve, he has an ability to envision it . . . He was just saying the other day that he is still working out ideas that he's had since he was 19 . . . that he would probably die before he could ever use them all."[1] When you bring that kind of ability to the team, how can it lose?

FLESHING IT OUT

Bob Taylor isn't a flashy guy. He's soft-spoken, and if you met him on the street, you probably wouldn't guess he owns a company that grossed $30 million in 1999.[2] But if you spent any time with him, you would almost instantly recognize his incredible competence.

The word *competent* sometimes is used to mean "barely adequate." When I talk about the quality of competence that is desirable in teammates, I mean it in the sense of its most basic definition, which means "to be well qualified, fit." Competent team members are very capable and highly qualified to do the job and do it well.

Highly competent people have some things in common:

1. They Are Committed to Excellence

John Johnson in *Christian Excellence* writes, "Success bases our worth on a comparison with others. Excellence gauges our value by measuring us against our own potential. Success grants its rewards to the few but is the dream of the multitudes. Excellence is available to all living beings but is accepted by the . . . few." The reason Bob Taylor says that you can let quality slip while accepting new people on the team is that his standards are already so high that a small slip doesn't hurt him much. He and his people are thoroughly committed to excellence.

> Success bases our worth on a comparison with others. Excellence gauges our value by measuring us against our own potential. Success grants its rewards to the few but is the dream of the multitudes. Excellence is available to all living beings but is accepted by the . . . few.
>
> —DALE CARNEGIE

2. They Never Settle for Average

The word *mediocre* literally means "halfway up a stony mountain." To be mediocre is to do a job halfway, to leave yourself far short of the summit. Competent people never settle for average. They focus their energy and efforts on what they do well, giving all they've got.

3. They Pay Attention to Detail

Dale Carnegie said, "Don't be afraid to give your best to what seemingly are small jobs. Every time you conquer one it makes you that much stronger. If you do little jobs well, the big ones tend to take care of themselves." When Bob started out making guitars, he did all the little jobs himself. Now he functions more as a team leader and designer of processes and manufacturing equipment. But he and his people still pay attention to the details. That has earned them the place they have achieved in the industry: Taylor is the largest producer of acoustic guitars in the world.

4. They Perform with Consistency

Highly competent people perform with great consistency. They give their best all the time, and that's important. If 99.9 percent were good enough, then 811,000 faulty rolls of 35 millimeter film would be loaded this year, 22,000 checks would be deducted from the wrong bank accounts in the next 60 minutes, and 12 babies would be given to the wrong parents today alone.[3]

I'm not a musician, but I'm told that if you try out a dozen identical instruments from most guitar manufacturers, you find some good ones, many average ones, and a few real stinkers. But a producer/songwriter friend says that if you pick up a Taylor guitar, there's never a bad one in the bunch. That's consistency.

REFLECTING ON IT

One of the things Bob Taylor says about himself is that he's good at "editing" himself. He does what he does well, continually persevering and distilling what's best—and he stops doing what he doesn't do well. Does that describe you? Do you focus your energy on what you can do well so that you become highly competent at it? Can your teammates depend on you to deliver in such a way that it brings the entire team success? If not, you may need to get better focused and develop the skills you need so that you can do your job and do it well.

BRINGING IT HOME

To improve your competence . . .

- *Focus yourself professionally.* It's hard to develop competence if you're trying to do everything. Pick an area in which to specialize. Bob believes he wouldn't be successful at anything but running Taylor Guitars. What is the one thing that brings together your skills, interests, and opportunities? Whatever it is, seize it.

- *Sweat the small stuff.* Too many people don't take their work as far as they can. To do that, you need to develop an ability to get all the details right. That doesn't mean becoming a micromanager or control freak. It means doing the last 10 percent of whatever job you're doing. Try doing that on the next project or big task that is your responsibility.

- *Give more attention to implementation.* Since implementation is often the most difficult part of any job, give it greater attention. How can you improve the gap between coming up with ideas and putting them into practice? Get your teammates together and discuss how you can improve the process.

DAILY TAKE-AWAY

A sea captain and a crusty chief engineer were talking one day, and they began to argue about whose expertise was most needed for the running of the ship. The debate got more and more heated, and finally the captain decided that they should trade jobs for a day. The chief engineer would be on the bridge, and the captain would go down to the engine room.

Only a few hours into their shift, the captain emerged from belowdecks sweating, his face and uniform covered with dirt and oil.

"Chief," he bellowed, "you need to get down to the engine room. I can't get her to go."

"Of course you can't," barked the chief. "She's aground!"

COMPANION
ONLINE
RESOURCE

Learn more about yourself and this quality of a team player by taking the FREE assessment at **QualitiesOfATeamPlayer.com**.

DEPENDABLE

TEAMS GO TO GO-TO PLAYERS

Fear not those who argue but those who dodge.

—*Wolfram Von Eschenbach*

Dependability is more than ability alone.

—*John C. Maxwell*

BUT WHOM DOES SUPERMAN DEPEND ON?

In 1995, Christopher Reeve had it all. He was married to his best friend, Dana. He had three wonderful children. And his family enjoyed a house and estate in beautiful Westchester County, New York.

It seemed that he could do anything he put his mind to. He was an accomplished pianist who had composed classical music. He was an avid outdoorsman and a superb athlete: an expert sailor, a licensed pilot, an excellent skier, a scuba diver, and a horseman.

And of course he experienced great success in his acting career. As a teenager, he had decided to pursue a career in show business, and by age sixteen, he had an agent. He attended Cornell University and the Juilliard School, learned his craft, and began getting work as a professional actor.

At the 1979 Academy Awards, John Wayne turned to Cary Grant and said of Reeve, "This is our new man. He's taking over [for us]."[1] Aided not only by his acting skills but also by his good looks and imposing physique at six feet four inches tall, he became a star. In 1995, at age forty-two, Reeve had performed in seventeen feature films (including the blockbuster *Superman*), a dozen movies for television, and about 150 plays. He was financially secure and had achieved critical acclaim. But then his life was turned upside down.

On May 27, 1995, during the cross-country portion of a riding competition, Christopher Reeve was thrown from his horse,

Buck. He crashed headfirst into the fence his horse refused to jump and then fell to the ground. He sustained an injury to his spine at the first and second vertebrae, and his breathing stopped. He was paralyzed from the neck down. If the paramedics hadn't arrived in minutes, he would not have lived.

Reeve has no memory of the fall. He remembers the time he spent in the stables a few minutes before his ride. The next thing he remembers is waking up a few days later in the intensive care unit of the University of Virginia. During those few intense days, doctors kept him alive with a respirator, stabilized him, and literally reattached his head to his spine surgically. The damage Reeve had sustained is sometimes called the hangman's injury. Reeve later quipped, "It was as if I'd been hanged, cut down and sent to rehab.[2]" He was given a 50 percent chance of surviving.

A serious spinal cord injury is difficult for any person to survive, emotionally as well as physically. An injury that leaves you helpless must be unfathomably devastating. But in the hours after he first woke up, he began to understand the real importance of a team.

"When they told me what my condition was, I felt that I was no longer a human being," he recalls. "Then Dana came into my room and knelt down to the level of my bed. We made eye contact. I said, 'Maybe this isn't worth it. Maybe I should just check out.' And she was crying, and she said, 'But you're still you, and I love you.' And that saved my life."[3]

Before the accident, Christopher and Dana Reeve had a good

marriage. But in the years since then, they have developed an even stronger partnership. Chris, Dana, and their son, Will, function as the core of that team, but they have also developed a wonderful larger team around them, consisting of an army of medical professionals. Some assist Chris with rigorous physical therapy, exercise, and respiratory therapy. Others feed, clothe, and bathe him, as well as help with other personal needs. Someone has to turn him over hourly each night as he sleeps. And he sees numerous specialists on a regular basis.

At first, the people around him simply kept him alive. But now they work to keep him healthy. "What you begin to say to yourself, instead of 'What life do I have?' is 'What life can I build?' And the answer, surprisingly, is, 'More than you think.'"[4]

Reeve hopes someday to walk again. Meanwhile, he understands his need for dependable people on his team. "If all the people who are around to help me were mad at me or in a lousy mood or whatever, and they went away," he observes, "there'd be nothing I could do about it. Absolutely nothing . . . It all comes down to goodwill. Nobody has to do any of those things; I'm completely dependent on them."[5] That's the way it is on every team, whether we can see it as clearly as Reeve does. Teammates must be able to depend on one another.

FLESHING IT OUT

Dependability may not always be a matter of life and death, as it is for Christopher Reeve, but it is certainly important to every team's success. You know it when you have people on your team upon whom you cannot depend. Everyone on the team knows it. Likewise, you know the ones you *can* depend on.

Allow me to note what I consider to be the essence of dependability:

1. *Pure Motives*

Aristotle believed that "all we do is done with an eye to something else." Evidently he believed that you can't trust anyone's motives. I don't agree with that. Most of the time I give people the benefit of the doubt. I try to keep my motives right, and I encourage my teammates to do likewise. However, if someone on the team continually puts himself and his agenda ahead of what's best for the team, he has proven himself to be undependable. When it comes to teamwork, motives matter.

2. *Responsibility*

Another quality of a dependable team player is a strong sense of responsibility. *New York Times* best-selling author and former editor Michael Korda emphasized, "In the final analysis, the one quality that all successful people have . . . is the ability to take on responsibility." While motivation addresses *why* people are dependable, responsibility indicates that they *want* to

> In the final analysis, the one quality that all successful people have . . . is the ability to take on responsibility.
>
> —MICHAEL KORDA

be dependable. That desire is described effectively by poet Edward Everett Hale, who wrote,

> I am only one,
> But still I am one.
> I cannot do everything
> But still I can do something;
> And because I cannot do everything
> I will not refuse to do the something that I can do.

Dependable team members possess the desire to do the things that they are capable of doing.

3. Sound Thinking

Gene Marine, the editor of the *Bellefontaine Examiner,* once sent a new sports reporter to cover an important game, but when the young man returned, he didn't have a story. Marine asked why, and the reporter replied simply, "No game."

"No game? What happened?" asked Marine.

"The stadium collapsed," responded the reporter.

"Then where is the story on the stadium collapse?" asked the editor.

"That wasn't my assignment, sir," answered the reporter. The potential for a news scoop went right down the tubes because of the young man's inability to think well.

Dependability means more than just wanting to take responsibility. That desire must also be coupled with good judgment to be of real value to the team.

4. Consistent Contribution

The final quality of a dependable team player is consistency. If you can't depend on teammates all the time, then you can't really depend on them any of the time. Consistency takes more than talent. It takes a depth of character that enables people to follow through—no matter how tired, distracted, or overwhelmed they are. As Britain's eloquent and steadfast prime minister of the last century, Winston Churchill, said, "It is not enough that we do our best; sometimes we have to do what's required."

> It is not enough that we do our best; sometimes we have to do what's required.
>
> —WINSTON CHURCHILL

REFLECTING ON IT

Are your teammates able to depend on you? Can they trust your motives? Do you make good decisions that others can rely on? And do you perform consistently, even when you don't feel like it? Are you a go-to player, or do your teammates work around you when crunch time comes?

BRINGING IT HOME

To improve your dependability . . .

- *Check your motives.* If you haven't committed goals to paper before, stop and do it before reading any farther. Now, look at those goals. How many of them benefit the teams you're part of—your family, the organization you work for, your fellow volunteers, the other players on your ball team? How many benefit only you personally? Spend some time working to align your personal priorities with those of your team.

- *Discover what your word is worth.* Approach five teammates with this question: "When I say that I intend to do something, how reliable am I? Rate me on a scale of one to ten." Include a superior and a subordinate in your survey, if possible. If the answers you get don't match your expectations, don't defend yourself. Simply ask for examples in a nonthreatening way. If the average answer is lower than a nine or ten, then start writing down your commitments as you make them from that day forward, and track your follow-through for one month.

- *Find someone to hold you accountable.* You are more likely to follow through and develop dependability if you have a partner to help you. Find someone you respect to help you keep your commitments.

DAILY TAKE-AWAY

In the mid-1800s during an economic depression, many state governments in the United States began to panic and started looking for solutions to their financial hardships. Pennsylvania, for example, simply declined to pay its debts in order to remain solvent, despite what many considered to be a relatively strong financial position.

When the legislature of the state of Ohio considered following Pennsylvania's example, Stephen Douglas, who eventually became a U.S. senator and ran unsuccessfully for president, resolved to try to prevent it. Unfortunately at the time he was deathly ill and restricted to his bed. But Douglas was determined. He had himself carried into the state legislature on a stretcher, and lying on his back, the "Little Giant," as he was known, spoke out against the policy. Due to his efforts, the legislature decided not to default on its obligations; instead, it met them. After the difficult economic times were over, the state prospered. It has been speculated that one of the reasons was that the government's dependability helped to set the stage for economic prosperity.

Never underestimate the long-reaching benefits that being dependable can bring.

COMPANION ONLINE RESOURCE

Learn more about yourself and this quality of a team player by taking the FREE assessment at **QualitiesOfATeamPlayer.com**.

7

DISCIPLINED

WHERE THERE'S A WILL, THERE'S A WIN

What we do on some great occasion will probably
depend on what we already are; and what we are
will be the result of previous years of self-discipline.

—H. P. Liddon

Discipline is the refining fire
by which talent becomes ability.

—Roy L. Smith

THE MAKING OF A WINNER

In his book *The Life God Blesses,* my friend Gordon MacDonald tells a story about his experiences on the track team at the University of Colorado in the late fifties. In particular, he remembers the difficult workouts he did with a teammate named Bill. "To this day I have anguished memories of our workouts each Monday afternoon," says Gordon. "The memories are onerous because the workouts were. When those Monday workouts ended, I would stagger in exhaustion to the locker room."

But Bill was different. Undoubtedly those workouts were demanding to him too. When he was finished, he would rest on the grass near the track. But after about twenty minutes, while Gordon showered, Bill would repeat the entire workout!

Bill didn't consider himself to be an exceptional athlete in college. During his years at the University of Colorado, he never earned a medal in national collegiate championship competition, nor was he named an All-American. "I was not a great athlete," observed Bill, "but I had the 'bag of tricks' theory . . . that is, there is no big move you can make in your training or in competition, but there are thousands of little things you can do."[1]

Bill might not have made a great impact during his college years, but his discipline and desire paid off over time. His best events were the long jump and the 400. He kept working on those and added other skills so that he could compete in the decathlon. Through disciplined effort and continual improvement, the un-spectacular college athlete who had worked out next to (and ahead of) Gordon MacDonald became a world-famous athlete. Bill was none other than Bill Toomey, the decathlete in-ducted into the Olympic Hall of Fame in 1984. He set a world record in the decathlon in 1966, won a gold medal in the Tokyo Olympics in 1968, and won five national decathlon champion-ships in a row—an accomplishment that has yet to be matched in his sport.

What elevated Toomey to such high accomplishment was his discipline. Gordon MacDonald's insight says it all: "The difference between the two of us began on Monday afternoons during workouts. He was unafraid of discipline and did the maximum; I was afraid of discipline and did the minimum."[2]

FLESHING IT OUT

Discipline is doing what you really don't want to do so that you can do what you really want to do. It's paying the price in the little things so that you can buy the bigger thing. And just as no individual succeeds without disci-

> **Discipline is doing what you really don't want to do so that you can do what you really want to do.**

pline, neither does any team. That's why it needs disciplined players. To become the kinds of players that teams want, people must develop discipline in three areas. They must possess . . .

1. Disciplined Thinking

You can't get far in life if you don't use your head. To do that, you don't have to be a genius; you just need to use the mind God has given you. Playwright George Bernard Shaw remarked, "Few people think more than two or three times a year; I have made an international reputation for myself by thinking once or twice a week." If you keep your mind active, regularly take on mental challenges, and continually think about the right things, you will develop the disciplined thinking that will help you with whatever you endeavor to do.

2. Disciplined Emotions

> People have just two choices when it comes to their emotions: they can master their emotions or be mastered by them.

People have just two choices when it comes to their emotions: they can master their emotions or be mastered by them. That doesn't mean that to be a good team player, you have to turn off your feelings. But it does mean that you shouldn't let your feelings prevent you from doing what you should or drive you to do things you shouldn't.

A classic example of what can happen when a person doesn't discipline his emotions can be seen in the life of golf legend Bobby Jones. Like today's Tiger Woods, Jones was a golf prodigy. He began playing in 1907 at age five. By age twelve, he was scoring below par, an accomplishment most golfers don't achieve in a lifetime of playing the game. At age fourteen, he qualified for the U.S. Amateur Championship. But Jones didn't win that event. His problem can be best described by the nickname he acquired: "club thrower." Jones often lost his temper—and his ability to play well.

An older golfer that Jones called Grandpa Bart advised the young man, "You'll never win until you can control that temper of yours." Jones took his advice and began working to discipline his emotions. At age twenty-one, Jones blossomed and went on to be one of the greatest golfers in history, retiring at age twenty-eight after winning the grand slam of golf. Grandpa Bart's comment sums up the situation: "Bobby was fourteen when he mastered the game of golf, but he was twenty-one when he mastered himself."

3. Disciplined Actions

Albert Hubert said, "Parties who want milk should not seat themselves on a stool in the middle of the field and hope that the cow will back up to them." Sharpening your mind and controlling your emotions are important, but they can take you only so far. Action separates the winners from the losers. The running back who does wind sprints, the attorney who reads up on cases, the doctor who keeps focused in the emergency room, the parent who comes home when promised instead

> Parties who want milk should not seat themselves on a stool in the middle of the field and hope that the cow will back up to them.
>
> —ALBERT HUBERT

of working later are all people practicing disciplined action. And when they do, the other people who are depending on them benefit.

REFLECTING ON IT

How are you doing when it comes to discipline? Do you take on mental and physical challenges just for the practice? Or are you constantly seeking a way to stay in your comfort zone? Do you sometimes regret that you've been unable to get yourself to do what you know to be right? Or most of the time do you believe that you do the best that you can? And how do you react under pressure? Do the people on your team expect extra effort or a sudden explosion from you when things go wrong? Your answers to those questions will give insight into whether you are winning the battle for discipline.

BRINGING IT HOME

To become a more disciplined team player . . .

• **Strengthen your work habits.** Biologist and educator Thomas Huxley remarked, "Perhaps the most valuable result of all education is the ability to make yourself do the thing you have to do, when it ought to be done, whether you like it or not; it is the first lesson that ought to be learned, and however early a man's training begins, it is probably the last lesson that he learns thoroughly." Discipline means doing the right things at the right time for the right reason. Review your priorities and follow-through to see if you're on track. And do something necessary but unpleasant every day to keep yourself disciplined.

> **Discipline means doing the right things at the right time for the right reason.**

- *Take on a challenge.* To strengthen your mind and resolve, pick a task or project that will put you in over your head. Doing that will require you to think sharply and act with discipline. Keep doing that and you will find yourself capable of more than you imagined.

- *Tame your tongue.* If you sometimes overreact emotionally, a first step to improvement is to stop yourself from saying things you shouldn't. The next time you want to lash out, hold your tongue for five minutes, and give yourself a chance to cool down and look at things more rationally. Use this strategy repeatedly and you will find yourself in better command of your emotions.

DAILY TAKE-AWAY

During the fourteenth century in what is now Belgium, there lived a man named Reynald III. Reynald was a nobleman, the rightful duke over his ancestral lands, but his younger brother revolted against him and usurped him. Reynald's brother needed the duke out of the way, but he didn't want to kill him. So he came up with an ingenious plan. Because Reynald was a very large man, his brother had him put into a room with a smaller-than-average door. If Reynald would simply lose some weight, he would be allowed to leave. In fact, the usurping brother promised that if Reynald left the room, his freedom and his title would be restored.

But Reynald was not a man of discipline, and his brother knew that. Every day, the brother had trays of delicious foods delivered to his older brother's room. And Reynald ate. In fact, instead of growing thinner, he grew fatter and fatter.

A person lacking discipline is in a prison without bars. Are your habits making a prisoner of you?

COMPANION ONLINE RESOURCE

Learn more about yourself and this quality of a team player by taking the FREE assessment at **QualitiesOfATeamPlayer.com**.

ENLARGING

ADDING VALUE TO TEAMMATES IS INVALUABLE

The purpose of life is not to win. The purpose of life is to grow and to share. When you come to look back on all that you have done in life, you will get more satisfaction from the pleasure you have brought to other people's lives than you will from the times that you outdid and defeated them.

—*Rabbi Harold Kushner*

Most of us plateau when we lose the tension between where we are and where we ought to be.

—*John Gardiner*

BRAVE HEART

In 1296, King Edward I of England assembled a large army and crossed the border of his own nation into Scotland. Edward was a skilled leader and fierce warrior. A tall, strong man, he had gained his first real combat experience beginning at age twenty-five. In the following years, he became a seasoned veteran while fighting in the Crusades in the Holy Lands.

At age fifty-seven, he was fresh from victories in Wales, whose people he'd crushed and whose land he'd annexed. In that conflict, his purpose had been clear: "to check the impetuous rashness of the Welsh, to punish their presumption and to wage war against them to their extermination."[1]

For a time, Edward had attempted to manipulate Scotland's fate. He managed to make himself overlord of the territory and then placed a weak king over it, a man the people of Scotland called Toom Tabard, meaning "empty coat." Then Edward bullied the straw king until he rebelled, thus giving the English monarch a reason to invade the country. The Scottish people crumpled.

Edward sacked the castle of Berwick and massacred its inhabitants. Other castles surrendered in quick succession. The Scottish king was stripped of power, and many believed that the fate of the Scots would be the same as that of the Welsh. But they didn't take into account the efforts of one man: Sir William Wallace, who is still revered as a national hero in Scotland even though he has been dead for nearly seven hundred years.

If you saw the movie *Braveheart,* then you have an image of William Wallace as a fierce and determined fighter who valued freedom above all else. His older brother, Malcolm, as the firstborn son, was expected to follow in the footsteps of their father as a warrior. William, as many second sons of the day, was being groomed for the clergy and was taught to value ideas, including freedom. But he grew to resent the oppressive English after his father was killed in an ambush and his mother was forced to live in exile. At age nineteen, he became a fighter when a group of Englishmen tried to bully him. By his early twenties, William was a highly skilled warrior.

During the time of William Wallace and Edward I, warfare was usually conducted by trained knights, professional soldiers, and sometimes hired mercenaries. The larger and more seasoned the army, the greater their power. When Edward faced the smaller Welsh army, they didn't stand a chance. And the same was expected of the Scots. But Wallace had an unusual ability. He drew the common people of Scotland to him, he made them believe in the cause of freedom, and he inspired and equipped them to fight against the professional war machine of England.

William Wallace was ultimately unable to defeat the English and gain Scotland's independence. At age thirty-three, he was brutally executed. (His treatment was actually worse than that portrayed in the movie *Braveheart.*) But his legacy of enlargement carried on. The next year, inspired by Wallace's example, nobleman Robert Bruce claimed the throne of Scotland and rallied not only the peasants but also the nobility. And in 1314, Scotland finally gained its hard-fought independence.

F L E S H I N G   I T   O U T

Team members always love and admire a player who is able to help them go to another level, someone who enlarges them and empowers them to be successful. Those kinds of people are like the Boston Celtics Hall of Fame center Bill Russell, who said, "The most important measure of how good a game I played was how much better I'd made my team-mates play."

> The most important measure of how good a game I played was how much better I'd made my teammates play.
>
> —BILL RUSSELL

Players who enlarge their teammates have several things in common:

1. Enlargers Value Their Teammates

Industrialist Charles Schwab observed, "I have yet to find the man, however exalted his station, who did not do better work and put forth greater effort under a spirit of approval than under a spirit of criticism." Your teammates can tell whether you believe in them. People's performances usually reflect the expectations of those they respect.

2. Enlargers Value What Their Teammates Value

Players who enlarge others do more than value their fellow team members; they understand what their teammates value. They listen to discover what their teammates talk about and watch to see what they spend their money on. That kind of knowledge, along with a desire to relate to their fellow players, creates a strong connection between teammates. And it makes possible an enlarger's next characteristic.

3. Enlargers Add Value to Their Teammates

Adding value is really the essence of enlarging others. It's finding ways to help others improve their abilities and attitudes. An enlarger looks for the gifts, talents, and uniqueness in other people, and then helps them to increase those abilities for their benefit and for that of the entire team. An enlarger is able to take others to a whole new level.

4. Enlargers Make Themselves More Valuable

Enlargers work to make themselves better, not only because it benefits them personally, but also because it helps them to help others. You cannot give what you do not have. For example, in basketball a great player like Karl Malone is aided by a great passer like all-time assist leader John Stockton. If you want to increase the ability of a teammate, make yourself better.

REFLECTING ON IT

How do your teammates see you? Are you an enlarger? Do you make them better than they are alone through your inspiration and contribution? Do you know what your teammates value?

Do you capitalize on those things by adding value to them in those areas?

Becoming an enlarger of others isn't always easy. First, it takes a secure person to add value to others. If you believe deep down that helping others somehow hurts you or your opportunities for success, then you'll have a hard time enlarging others. But as Henry Ward Beecher insisted, "No man is more cheated than the selfish man." When a team member unselfishly enlarges others, he also enlarges himself.

> **No man is more cheated than the selfish man.**
> —HENRY WARD BEECHER

Bringing It Home

If you want to be an enlarging team player, then do the following:

- *Believe in others before they believe in you.* If you want to help people become better, you need to become an initiator. You can't hold back. Ask yourself, *What is special, unique, and wonderful about that teammate?* Then share your observations with the person and with others. If you believe in others and give them a positive reputation to uphold, you can help them to become better than they think they are.

- *Serve others before they serve you.* One of the most beneficial services you can perform is helping other human beings to reach their potential. In your family, serve your spouse.

Free up time and resources for enriching experiences. On the ball field, find a way to get your teammate the ball. In business, help your colleagues to shine. And whenever possible, give credit to others for the team's success.

- *Add value to others before they add value to you.* A basic truth of life is that people will always move toward anyone who increases them and away from others who devalue them. You can enlarge others by pointing out their strengths and helping them to focus on improvement. But remember this: encourage and motivate people out of their comfort zone, but never out of their gift zone. If you try to push people to work in areas where they have no talent, you will only frustrate them.

> **People will always move toward anyone who increases them and away from others who devalue them.**

DAILY TAKE-AWAY

For as long as he could remember, a boy named Chris Greicius dreamed of someday becoming a police officer. But there was a major obstacle standing in his way. He had leukemia, and he was not expected to make it to adulthood. When he was seven years old, Chris's battle with the disease took a turn for the worse, and that's when a family friend, who was a U.S. customs officer, arranged for Chris to come as close as he could to living his dream.

He made a call to Officer Ron Cox in Phoenix and arranged for Chris to spend the day with officers from the Arizona Department of Public Safety.

When the day arrived, Chris was welcomed by three squad cars and a police motorcycle ridden by Frank Shankwitz. Then he was treated to a ride in a police helicopter. They finished the day by swearing Chris in as the first—and only—honorary state trooper. The next day, Cox enlisted the assistance of the company that manufactured the uniforms for the Arizona Highway Patrol, and within twenty-four hours, their people presented Chris with an official patrolman's uniform. He was ecstatic.

Two days later, Chris died in the hospital, his uniform close at hand. Officer Shankwitz was saddened by his little friend's death, but he was grateful that he had experienced the opportunity to help Chris. And he also realized that there were many children in circumstances similar to Chris's. That prompted Shankwitz to cofound the Make-A-Wish Foundation. In twenty years since then, he and his organization have enlarged the experiences of more than eighty thousand children.

There is nothing as valuable—or rewarding—as adding value to the lives of others.

COMPANION
ONLINE
RESOURCE

Learn more about yourself and this quality of a team player by taking the FREE assessment at **QualitiesOfATeamPlayer.com**.

9

ENTHUSIASTIC

YOUR HEART IS THE SOURCE
OF ENERGY FOR THE TEAM

I feel sorry for the person who can't get genuinely
excited about his work. Not only will he never be satisfied,
but he will never achieve anything worthwhile.

—*Walter Chrysler*

Nothing great was ever achieved without enthusiasm.

—*Ralph Waldo Emerson*

HOG LOVERS

Their passion is legendary, just as the object of their passion is. Many of them are members of an organization called HOG. And in June of 1998, more than 140,000 of them rode through the streets of Milwaukee, Wisconsin, to celebrate their love. They are owners of Harley-Davidson motorcycles.

June of 1998 marked the ninety-fifth anniversary of the Harley-Davidson Motor Company, an organization that began when twenty-one-year-old William S. Harley and his twenty-year-old friend Arthur Davidson decided to motorize bicycles in a small wooden shed in 1903. That first year they hand-built and sold three motorcycles. It didn't take them long to find success and to expand their enterprise. Each year they produced more vehicles.

As motorcycle racing came into existence and gained popularity, Harley-Davidson dominated. When World War I broke out, the Allies quickly discovered the value of motorcycles in the war effort. Harley-Davidson estimates that the company provided most of the twenty thousand motorcycles used by the U.S. Army in the war. And after the armistice was signed, the first American to enter Germany did so on a Harley-Davidson motorcycle.[1]

For more than half a century, the company thrived. One of its strengths was that it was a family-owned business whose employees and customers felt connected by their love for Harley-Davidson motorcycles. And the company continued to grow, to update and improve their motorcycles, and to gain fans. By the early 1970s, Harley-Davidson owned nearly 80 percent of the large-motorcycle (850+ cc) market in the United States.[2]

But even before Harley-Davidson reached their peak in the seventies, they began to have major problems. In the early 1960s, the company went public to raise funds so that it could modernize, diversify, and better compete against Japanese manufacturers. In the late 1960s, AMF acquired the firm. After a proud sixty-five-year history in Milwaukee, the company's headquarters was abruptly moved to New York, and vehicle final assembly was moved to Pennsylvania. The people on Harley-Davidson's staff were demoralized.

Over the next decade, Harley-Davidson's reputation slid. The motorcycles became notoriously unreliable. Police officers in departments around the country who were once proud to ride the company's American-made vehicles began to buy Japanese products, which were cheaper and more dependable. By 1980, Harley-Davidson possessed slightly more than 30 percent of a market that it had once dominated. And for the first time in its history, the company lost money. Harley-Davidson's future looked grim.

The thing that saved Harley-Davidson was one of the things it always had going for it: the passion of employees and customers for the motorcycle that bore the company's name. In 1981, thirteen senior executives of the company bought the company, including Vaughn Beals, a Harley enthusiast since World War II who ran the motorcycle division for AMF. They quickly began to turn Harley-Davidson around. They streamlined operations, improved manufacturing methods, and introduced new products. They also harnessed the enthusiasm of Harley owners by creating HOG, the Harley Owners Group (which has more than six hundred thousand members today). In 1985, Harley-Davidson earned a profit for the first time in five years.

A lot of people left the company during those years, but the employees who stayed were dedicated. In the years to follow, Harley-Davidson decided to harness their commitment, knowledge, and enthusiasm in a unique partnership that began between labor and management and then expanded to include all of what the company identifies as its various stakeholders: customers, employees, suppliers, shareholders, government, and society. Today the enthusiasm and partnership are paying off. Harley-Davidson manufactures and sells more than two hundred thousand vehicles in countries around the world every year with net sales of more than $2.9 billion.[3]

FLESHING IT OUT

What saved Harley-Davidson? I believe it was enthusiasm. It was the enthusiasm of Beals and the other twelve executives who bought the company and kept it from going under in 1981. It was the enthusiasm of the employees who stayed with the company under difficult circumstances in order to produce better motorcycles as 40 percent of the organization's workforce was

> People can succeed at almost anything for which they have enthusiasm.
>
> —CHARLES SCHWAB

74

cut. And of course it was the enthusiasm of the customers—who have long considered a Harley-Davidson to be the pinnacle of motorcycles—that has made the company the financial success it is today.

There is no substitute for enthusiasm. When the members of a team are enthusiastic, the whole team becomes highly energized. And that energy produces power. Industrialist Charles Schwab observed, "People can succeed at almost anything for which they have enthusiasm."

Think about people who bring an enthusiastic attitude to teamwork and you will realize that they . . .

1. Take Responsibility for Their Own Enthusiasm

Successful people understand that attitude is a choice—and that includes enthusiasm. People who wait for external forces to help them spark their enthusiasm are at other people's mercy all the time. They are likely to run hot or cold based on what's going on around them at any given moment. However, positive people are positive because they choose to be. If you want to be positive, upbeat, and passionate, you need to take responsibility for being that way.

> **Positive people are positive because they choose to be.**

2. Act Their Way into Feeling

You cannot win if you do not begin. That's one of the reasons why you need to act your way into feeling. You can't break a cycle of apathy by waiting to *feel* like doing it. I addressed an issue similar to this in *Failing Forward:*

> People who want to get out of the fear cycle often . . . believe that they have to eliminate [their fear] to break the cycle. But . . . you can't wait for motivation to get you going. To conquer fear, you have to feel the fear and take action anyway . . . You've got to get yourself moving. The only way to break the cycle is to face your fear and take action—no matter how small or seemingly insignificant that action might seem. To get over fear, you've got to get started.[4]

Likewise, if you want to be enthusiastic, you need to start acting that way. If you wait for the feeling before acting, you may never become enthusiastic.

3. Believe in What They Do

So how do people who don't *feel* enthusiastic engender enthusiasm? One of the best ways is to think about all the positive aspects of your work. Believing in what you do and focusing on those positive beliefs will help you to act and to speak positively about what you're doing. That helps to spark the fire of enthusiasm inside you, and once that starts, all you need to do is to keep feeding the flames.

4. Spend Time with Other Enthusiastic People

If you want to augment your enthusiasm, hang around enthusiastic people. The author of books on the psychology of winning, Denis Waitley, says, "Enthusiasm is contagious. It's difficult to remain neutral or indifferent in the presence of a positive thinker." And when you put together a whole team of enthusiastic people, the possibilities for that team are endless.

> **Enthusiasm is contagious. It's difficult to remain neutral or indifferent in the presence of a positive thinker.**
>
> **—DENIS WAITLEY**

REFLECTING ON IT

Microsoft chairman Bill Gates remarked, "What I do best is share my enthusiasm." Obviously that ability has brought the people in his organization immense success. If asked, would your teammates say that you have a similar effect on them? Enthusiasm increases a person's accomplishments while apathy increases his alibis. Which are people more likely to discover in you?

BRINGING IT HOME

To improve your enthusiasm . . .

- *Show a sense of urgency.* A good way to fire up your own furnace is to do things with greater urgency. Identify a project that you are currently less enthusiastic about than you should be. Give yourself deadlines for completing its steps that are a little more ambitious than you feel comfortable with. Doing that should help you be more focused and energized.

- *Be willing to do more.* One way to demonstrate enthusiasm with your teammates is to go the extra mile with others. This week when someone asks you to do something, do what's required and then some. Then quietly observe its impact on the team's atmosphere.

- *Strive for excellence.* Elbert Hubbard said, "The best preparation for good work tomorrow is to do good work today." Nothing breeds enthusiasm like a job well done. If you've allowed yourself to ease off when it comes to your work standards, redouble efforts to do things according to your highest levels of excellence.

> The best preparation for good work tomorrow is to do good work today.
>
> —ELBERT HUBBARD

DAILY TAKE-AWAY

They donate time every month to something that will ultimately last only a few hours. They work every New Year's Eve and New Year's Day, volunteering their time instead of going to parties or staying home with their families. They are the men and women who build and decorate the floats for the annual Tournament of Roses Parade in Pasadena, California.

Each year, more than 1 million people line the parade route, and more than 400 million people tune in via television to watch the colorful flower-covered floats of the parade that has been held every year since 1890. Though many of the floats are now created and produced by professional float-building companies, some are still designed and built by volunteers. Float construction goes on from spring to December. And then the entire float has to be decorated with flowers, seeds, and other natural objects in the days just before the parade.

"It's a lot of work, a lot of volunteers," a float coordinator explains. "[It takes] about 4,000 man hours to actually build a float, and probably equally as many hours to decorate a float."

What keeps people coming back to volunteer as members of a float team year after year? Their enthusiasm. Volunteer Pam Kontra explains, "It is a lot of fun. It's a lot of work, and it's a lot of time, but to see [a float] rolling down the road and saying, 'I worked right there on that part!', is like so exciting to see."[5] That kind of enthusiasm gives an individual—and a team—the energy required to accomplish even the most difficult tasks.

COMPANION ONLINE RESOURCE

Learn more about yourself and this quality of a team player by taking the FREE assessment at **QualitiesOfATeamPlayer.com**.

10

INTENTIONAL

MAKE EVERY ACTION COUNT

It is easy in the world to live after the world's opinions;
it is easy in solitude to live after your own;
but the great man is he who in the midst of the crowd
keeps with perfect sweetness the independence of solitude.

—*Ralph Waldo Emerson*

You've got to think about "big things" while you're
doing small things, so that all the small things go in
the right direction.

—*Alvin Toffler*

WHAT A DOLL!

In 2000, my wife, Margaret, and I became grandparents. Our daughter, Elizabeth, and her husband, Steve, brought a girl named Madeline into the world, and then a few months later our son, Joel Porter, and his wife, Elisabeth (yes, it does confuse us too!), brought us a girl named Hannah. For years, friends with grandchildren had told us how great it is being a grandparent. It's all that they claimed and more.

Margaret and I now have a new pastime: searching for books, toys, and gifts for those two children. One day Margaret came home and said, "John, I just found the most wonderful things for the girls. They're not old enough yet, but it's a series of books that teaches about American history from the point of view of a girl."

She showed me a catalog. "It's called the American Girls Collection," she continued. "Each group of books is set in a different time period in American history. There are dolls for each book series, period clothes, accessories, and other things. There's even a magazine the girls will be able to get."

The whole series sounded like a wonderful thing for our granddaughters. I became intrigued, too, not just because of my grandchildren, but because I was impressed with the company. So I started to do some research.

What I discovered was an organization called Pleasant Company that was founded in 1986 by Pleasant T. Rowland, a former teacher. In the classroom, Rowland had been frustrated by the uncreative textbooks she was given, so she began developing her own materials. Later, she worked in educational research and publishing. Eventually she began her own company when she and friend Valerie Tripp came up with a creative idea for girls. Rowland says, "As an educator, I wanted to give girls an understanding of America's past and a sense of pride in the traditions they share with girls of yesterday. Out of this desire, The American Girls Collection was born."[1]

At the heart of the collection are the books. The process of bringing the books together is complicated, and it requires a high degree of intentionality every step of the way. First, Pleasant Company editors create a proposal for a character to be set in a particular time period and location. It includes information on the period's significance to American history and how girls today will relate to it. It examines the culture, including housing, clothing, food, and more. It also identifies possible experts, authors, and illustrators who could work on the project. Once every department has reviewed the potential project, the editors choose an author, and the project development department begins researching products that could be created to enrich the learning process for children.

Obviously the strategy has worked. The company has been highly successful, both educationally and financially. So far, the company has sold 61 million books and 5 million dolls, and its magazine has 700,000 subscribers.[2] And Pleasant Rowland has received numerous awards and honors, such as recognition by the Institute of American Entrepreneurs (on whose board she now serves).

Since Rowland is an entrepreneur, perhaps her greatest recognition came when her company was acquired by Mattel in 1998 and she became Mattel's vice chairman. Undoubtedly Mattel's decision makers were impressed by her business skill, sense of mission, and ability to turn her vision into reality by making every move count through intentional leadership.

F L E S H I N G   I T   O U T

What does it mean to be intentional? It means working with purpose—making every action count. In Chapter 11, we're going to talk about being mission conscious, which relates to keeping the big picture in mind. But being intentional is different. It's about focusing on doing the right things, moment to moment, day to day, and then following through with them in a consistent way.

Successful individuals are intentional. They aren't scattered or haphazard. They know what they're doing and why they're doing it. For a team to be successful, it needs intentional people who are able to remain focused and productive, people who make every action count.

Anyone who desires to live with intentionality will have to do the following:

1. Have a Purpose Worth Living For

Being intentional begins with a sense of purpose. Willis R. Whitney, the first director of General Electric's research laboratory,

> **Some men have thousands of reasons why they cannot do what they want to, when all they need is one reason why they can.**
>
> —WILLIS R. WHITNEY

offered this thought: "Some men have thousands of reasons why they cannot do what they want to, when all they need is one reason why they can." You can see that one strong reason at work in the life and work of Pleasant Rowland. Her goal was to educate children and particularly to help girls. That desire became a guide to her actions and helped her to build a $300 million company. You can't be intentional if you don't have a strong sense of purpose.

2. *Know Your Strengths and Weaknesses*

Filmmaker Woody Allen remarked, "No matter what I'm working on, I like to do what I'm not doing." While he may not love *every* aspect of his profession, he has made so many movies that he must enjoy most parts of it. And he's good at it too. The truth is that people like to do what they're good at. Playing to your strengths rekindles your passions and renews your energy. If you know yourself and what you do well, then you can direct your time and energy in an intentional way.

3. *Prioritize Your Responsibilities*

Once you know the *why* of your life, it becomes much easier to figure out the *what* and *when*. *Walden* author Henry David

Thoreau observed, "One is not born into the world to do everything, but to do something." That means knowing your priorities and working according to them continually.

> **One is not born into the world to do everything, but to do something.**
> —HENRY DAVID THOREAU

4. Learn to Say No

Another thing an intentional person has to learn is how to say no. For me, that has been really difficult. I never met an opportunity I didn't like, so my natural desire is to say yes to everything. But you can't accomplish much without focus.

Chemist John A. Widtsoe said, "Let every man sing his own song in life." If you try to do every good thing that comes your way, you won't excel at what you were made to do.

5. Commit Yourself to Long-Term Achievement

A short-term, all-or-nothing approach to life works against many people. They have a kind of lottery mind-set: either they want to win big, or they don't want to make any effort at all. However, most victories in life are achieved through small, incremental wins sustained over time. Being willing to dedicate yourself long term to the process of achievement, instead of to its immediate rewards, will enable you to be more intentional. That's true when it comes to personal growth, relationship building, financial investment, or professional success.

REFLECTING ON IT

How intentional are you? As you proceed through your day, do you have a plan and a purpose for everything you do? Do you know where you're going and why you're doing what you're doing? Or are you simply drifting down the stream of life? If your teammates don't detect a sense of intentionality in you, they won't know what to expect from you, and they will be unlikely to count on you when it really counts.

BRINGING IT HOME

To improve your intentionality . . .

- *Explore your strengths and weaknesses.* You can't be intentional and effectively focused if you don't know yourself. If you've not done much self-examination, take an inventory of your strengths and weaknesses. Then survey family members, friends, and colleagues for additional insight. The more information and honest feedback you can get, the better.

- *Specialize in your specialty.* When you have a solid understanding of your strengths, you will be able to focus. Your goal should be to spend 80 percent of your time and effort on what brings high return to you and your team. Adjust your daily schedule and to-do list as much as possible to conform to that standard.

- *Plan your calendar with purpose.* The longer the time period you can plan with intentionality, the more you can get done. If you think in terms of a few hours or a single day, there's only so much you can do. You're better off thinking in terms of what you want to get done in a week or a month. (It's also a good idea to give yourself annual goals.) Set aside time this week to plan your activities in a longer block of time than you're accustomed to doing. If you're used to thinking daily, then plan for a week. If you usually plan weekly, then work out your goals for a month. It will help you to be more intentional throughout your days.

DAILY TAKE-AWAY

My friend Dwight Bain sent me a story of a ham radio operator who one day overheard an older gentleman giving advice to a younger man on the air.

"It's a shame you have to be away from home and your family so much," he said. "Let me tell you something that has helped me keep a good perspective on my own priorities. You see, one day I sat down and did a little arithmetic. The average person lives about seventy-five years. Now then, I multiplied 75 times 52 and came up with 3,900, which is the number of Saturdays that the average person has in his lifetime.

"It took me until I was fifty-five years old to think about all this in any detail," he continued, "and by that time I had lived through over 2,800 Saturdays. I got to thinking that if I lived to be seventy-five, I only had about a thousand of them left to enjoy."

He went on to explain that he bought 1,000 marbles and put them in a clear plastic container in his favorite work area at home. "Every Saturday since then," he said, "I have taken one marble out and thrown it away. I found that by watching the marbles diminish, I focused more on the really important things in life. There's nothing like watching your time here on this earth run out to help get your priorities straight."

Then the older gentleman finished, "Now let me tell you one last thought before I sign off and take my lovely wife out to breakfast. This morning, I took the very last marble out of the container. I figure if I make it until next Saturday, then I have been given a little extra time."

We can't choose whether we will get any more time, but we can choose what we do with it. If you are intentional with what you have, then you will make the most of the time and talent that God gives you.

COMPANION **ONLINE** RESOURCE

Learn more about yourself and this quality of a team player by taking the FREE assessment at **QualitiesOfATeamPlayer.com**.

11

MISSION CONSCIOUS

THE (BIG) PICTURE IS COMING IN LOUD AND CLEAR

The secret of success is constancy to purpose.

—Benjamin Disraeli

He who has a "why" to live for
can bear almost any "how."

—Friedrich Nietzsche

STICKING TO HER GUNS

It was particularly hot and humid on June 28, 1778, near the Monmouth Courthouse in the town of Freehold, New Jersey. That was the day during the American Revolutionary War that General George Washington, who had spent most of the war waging a battle of strategy and movement against the British, finally determined to fight the enemy in a full engagement.

After a tentative attack and withdrawal by American general Charles Lee, the revolutionary forces rallied under General Washington and engaged in a fierce artillery battle against the British. It turned out to be the largest and longest battle of that type staged during the Revolutionary War. For hours, in heat that approached nearly 100 degrees, the two opposing artillery groups hurled tons of shells and iron shot at one another. Each side fought using ten guns, and for a long time neither side gained the advantage.

As the men fought on, exhaustion threatened to overcome them, and many of them called for water. Mary Hays, the wife of artilleryman William Hays, rushed to the front lines with water to help the soldiers keep fighting. It was the kind of thing she had done before. She had traveled with her husband throughout the war, as many spouses did in those days. She cooked, helped to look after the men, and even tended to the wounded during battles. She was as dedicated to the cause of freedom and the defeat of the British as any soldier in the Continental army. She had even suffered through the horrible winter at Valley Forge with the army.

On this day, because of the heat, fetching water was a full-time job, although she did help with the wounded as well. After she returned to the battle line from one of her trips to a stream, she noticed that her husband, William, who had been relieved from his gun so that he could rest, was back in the fight because the man who had replaced him had been wounded. The battle was so even that the Americans couldn't afford to have a single cannon out of commission for fear of losing the battle.

As Mary watched, her husband was also struck down by enemy fire. He was dead. She didn't hesitate. Mary had been with the army long enough to know what must be done. With the battery short of gunners, she stepped forward and took her husband's place as the cannon's gunner.

A Connecticut soldier described Mary's actions during the battle in his autobiography:

> While in the act of reaching a cartridge and having one of her feet as far before the other as she could step, a cannon shot from the enemy passed directly between her legs without doing any other damage than carrying away all the lower part of her petticoat. Looking at it with apparent unconcern, she . . . continued her occupation.[1]

After hours of fighting, the British artillery was forced to withdraw. The Continental army had won the battle.

Though it was not considered a major military victory, the Battle of Monmouth was a political triumph and a tremendous morale booster for the revolutionaries. The Continental army had faced the British in the open field and forced them to retreat. And in this longest of battles of the American Revolution, the British had suffered two to three times more casualties than their American counterparts. For her actions in the battle, Mary Hays was issued a warrant as a noncommissioned officer by General George Washington.

FLESHING IT OUT

Mary Hays, who has come to be known as "Molly Pitcher" in history books, is symbolic of the attitude of many of the people who fought in the American Revolution. They were highly mission conscious, and that sense of purpose and mission continually drove them to do what was best for their cause, their fellow fighters, and their nation.

Not many of us can relate to the battlefield heroics of someone like Mary Hays, but we can certainly embrace the mission-conscious attitude she brought to her team. She exhibited the four qualities of all mission-conscious players:

1. They Know Where the Team Is Going

As Americans, we admire the people who founded our nation. We respect their courage, commitment, and sacrifice. We also admire their sense of vision and mission. They knew they were fighting for freedom and the future of a country that had the potential to give its people great opportunities. There is immense power in a sense of mission. Author W. Clement Stone stated, "When you discover your mission, you will feel its demand. It will fill you with enthusiasm and a burning desire to get to work on it." That sense of desire—and direction—is as indispensable for a team to be successful as it is for any individual.

2. They Let the Leader of the Team Lead

Mission-conscious team players who have committed themselves to a team allow the leader of the team to do the leading. Ironically the American army almost lost the Battle of Monmouth because of the actions of one of its own generals: Charles Lee. Commander in Chief George Washington, ordered Lee to attack the British and to harass them until the full force of the American army could engage them. Lee, who opposed Washington's plan, advanced tentatively and then suddenly retreated without cause. Lee nearly lost the Americans the opportunity to engage and defeat the enemy.

Fortunately Washington was able to take over his subordinate's command, but Lee was ultimately relieved of his command following a court-martial.

> **Leadership is the capacity to translate vision into reality.**
> —WARREN G. BENNIS

Any time a team member hinders the leader, it increases the possibility that the team will be hindered in its goals. However, mission-conscious players understand what leadership expert Warren G. Bennis articulated: "Leadership is the capacity to translate vision into reality." For a team to win, the leader must be allowed to lead.

3. They Place Team Accomplishment Ahead of Their Own

Teamwork always requires sacrifice. Good team players put team accomplishment ahead of what they can accomplish personally because that's what it takes to achieve the team's mission of the team. Often that means sacrificing personal goals or even personal safety, as was the case for Mary Hays. In the heat of battle, she didn't even allow herself to grieve for her lost husband. The stakes were too high for her to do anything but serve the team.

4. They Do Whatever Is Necessary to Achieve the Mission

It's obvious that Mary Hays was willing to do whatever it took to achieve the mission of her team, whether it was the common duties of a woman who traveled with the army, such as cooking, washing clothes, or serving, or the duties beyond her typical role, such as stepping into the battle lines with the soldiers. Mission-conscious team players today should have the same kind of attitude that Mary had. If success can come to the team only by your compromising, trying something new, or putting your agenda on hold, then that's what you need to do.

REFLECTING ON IT

Do you and your teammates keep the big picture in mind? Are you continually looking for ways to help the team realize its mission? Or do you tend to get so bogged down in the details of your responsibilities that you lose sight of the big picture? If you in any way hinder the bigger team—your organization—because of your desire to achieve personal success or even the success of your department, then you may need to take steps to improve your ability to keep the team's mission in mind.

BRINGING IT HOME

To improve your mission consciousness . . .

- **Check to see if your team focuses on its mission.** It's difficult to maintain a mission-conscious mind-set on a team that lacks a mission. Truthfully a team isn't

> **A team isn't really a team if it isn't going anywhere!**

really a team if it isn't going anywhere! So start by measuring the clarity of the mission. Does your team or organization have a mission statement? If not, work to get the team to create one. If it does, then examine whether the goals of the team match its mission. If the values, mission, goals, and practices of a team don't match up, you're going to have a tough time as a team player.

- **Find ways to keep the mission in mind.** If you're a strong achiever, the type of person who is used to working alone, or you tend to focus on the immediate rather than the big picture, you may need extra help being reminded of the mission of the team. Write down the mission and place it somewhere you can see it. Put it on an index card on your bathroom mirror, make it a message on your computer's screen saver, or have it made into a plaque for your desk. Keep it in front of you so that you are always conscious of the team's mission.

- *Contribute your best as a team member.* Once you're sure of the team's mission and direction, determine to contribute your best in the context of the team, not as an individual. That may mean taking a behind-the-scenes role for a while. Or it may mean focusing your inner circle in a way that contributes more to the organization, even if it gives you and your people less recognition.

DAILY TAKE-AWAY

For twenty years, one of the most productive players in baseball was Reggie Jackson. Now a member of the Major League Baseball Hall of Fame in Cooperstown, New York, Jackson was called "Mr. October" for his legendary prowess as a batter during the play-off and World Series games in which he played.

In *How Life Imitates the World Series,* Thomas Boswell tells how Jackson, who was then with the Baltimore Orioles, once stole a base in a game without having been given the sign to do so. That was something that manager Earl Weaver didn't allow. But Jackson, who has never lacked self-confidence, did it anyway. He was a good runner, and he believed that he knew the pitchers and catchers against whom he was playing so well that he could judge whether or not he should steal.

Later, Weaver took Jackson aside and explained why he hadn't wanted him to steal. The next batter in the order was Lee May, a powerful hitter. With first base open and the chance of May hitting into a double play now gone, the opposing pitcher intentionally walked May. That brought up the next player in the batting order, a man who had a poor record against that particular pitcher. Weaver then had to send in a pinch hitter to try to get Jackson and May around the bases to score. As a result, he didn't have that pinch hitter available later in the game when he really needed him.

Although Jackson was right in his assessment of his skill against the opposing team, he hurt the team. Why? Because he had his own achievement in mind and not the big picture when making a decision that affected the whole team. Good team players see more than the details of the moment. They are always conscious of a team's mission and act to help achieve it.

COMPANION ONLINE RESOURCE

Learn more about yourself and this quality of a team player by taking the FREE assessment at **QualitiesOfATeamPlayer.com**.

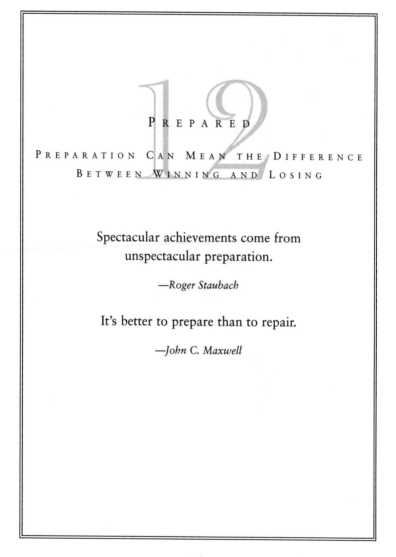

12

PREPARED

PREPARATION CAN MEAN THE DIFFERENCE BETWEEN WINNING AND LOSING

Spectacular achievements come from
unspectacular preparation.

—*Roger Staubach*

It's better to prepare than to repair.

—*John C. Maxwell*

CONSCIENTIOUS HERO

Alvin York is called the greatest soldier of World War I. For his actions during the Battle of the Argonne, York, an uneducated mountain boy from rural Tennessee, received the Distinguished Service Cross, the Croix de Guerre and Legion of Honor from France, the Croce di Guerra from Italy, the War Medal of Montenegro, and the Medal of Honor, the United States' highest decoration. At his medal ceremony French commander Marshal Ferdinand Foch said to York, "What you did was the greatest thing ever accomplished by any soldier of any of the armies of Europe."[1]

Before the war, nobody would have anticipated that York would become a hero—not even York himself! The third of eleven children, he grew up in the mountains of Tennessee. Like his father, he farmed, worked as an unskilled laborer, and took some work as a blacksmith. But his first love was hunting. And like his father and most of the men in the rural valley where he grew up, he was a crack shot.

When York was twenty-four years old, his father died, and he became the family's primary provider. However, after a year or two, York started to spend much time drinking, gambling, and fighting. He soon developed a reputation as someone who "would never amount to anything."[2] But on New Year's Day of 1915, when he was twenty-seven years old, York decided to change. He promised his mother he would turn his life around, and later that winter at a revival meeting, York became a man of faith by giving his life to Christ.

During the next two years, Alvin York became a different person. He altogether stopped drinking, using tobacco, swearing, and fighting. He worked hard to support his family. He studied the Bible. And he helped to found a church in his town where he became the second elder and worship leader. He also embraced the small denomination's stance against war. So when he received a draft notice in 1917, he was in a dilemma. He loved his country, and his family had fought for it all the way back to colonial times. But he also loved God and wanted to obey Him. York wrote,

> You see my religion and my experience . . . told me not to go to war, and the memory of my ancestors . . . told me to get my gun and go fight . . . It was a most awful thing when the wishes of your God and your country . . . get mixed up and go against each other . . . I wanted to be a good Christian and a good American too.[3]

At first, York was classified as a conscientious objector. And though he had not yet resolved whether he would fight, York did go off to army basic training at Camp Gordon, Georgia, when he was ordered to. And there he excelled. York was a natural leader, and his early life had prepared him well to be a soldier. He was physically strong, he was disciplined, and he was deadly accurate with a rifle at two hundred yards.

The only area where York was not prepared was in his heart. He still wasn't sure whether he could take another person's life.

So he endeavored to work through the issue. He consulted repeatedly with his pastor. He discussed the dilemma with his captain and his major. He wrestled with it from November 14 when he was inducted into the army until April 30, right before he was shipped overseas. And finally he came to a conclusion. Knowing the Bible said that peacemakers are blessed, York determined, "If a man can make peace by fighting, he is a peacemaker."[4] That completed his preparation—not only physically and mentally but also spiritually.

Although York saw action in France beginning in June, it wasn't until October 8, 1918, that he performed the acts that made him a hero. During the Battle of the Argonne, when a group of American soldiers from his company got pinned down by German machine-gun fire, seventeen men including York were sent across enemy lines to create a distraction. The men soon found themselves overrunning a camp of more than twenty German soldiers who had set their weapons aside to eat. The Americans took the Germans prisoner, but upon a word from a German officer, the machine guns along the front swiveled and suddenly turned on them. In seconds, all but eight of the Americans were dead or wounded, including all the non-commissioned officers. That left York, a corporal, in command.

For more than two decades, York had hunted or competed in weekly shooting contests in his hometown of Pall Mall, Tennessee. That preparation served him well that day against the machine gunners. As they would stand up to fire on the Americans, York would take them out one by one. After shooting several, he tried to get them to give up, but they wouldn't. He killed seventeen men with seventeen shots, eliminating the threat of the machine-gun nest.

When York ran out of rifle ammunition, a group of Germans charged him with bayonets. He defended himself with his pistol, felling eight men with eight shots. Afterward, as York and the others marched their prisoners back, they continued to take captive other German soldiers and officers. By the time they returned to Allied territory, the eight Americans had taken 132 German prisoners. York's preparation and cool head under fire had saved his squad and helped secure a major victory for the Allies.

York came home to a New York City ticker-tape parade, fame, and numerous lucrative endorsement offers. But York's desire was to help school uneducated children in his community. York wrote, "I kind of figured my trials and tribulations in the war had been to prepare me for doing just this work in the mountains. All my sufferings in having to go and kill were to teach me the value of human lives. All the temptations I went through were to strengthen my character."[5] In 1926, he helped to establish the York Agricultural Institute, which is still teaching students today.

FLESHING IT OUT

Spanish novelist Miguel de Cervantes stated, "The man who is prepared has his battle half-fought." That was true for Alvin

York, and it can be true for you. If you want to prepare yourself so that you can help your team as it faces the challenges ahead, then think about the following:

> **The man who is prepared has his battle half-fought.**
> —MIGUEL DE CERVANTES

1. Assessment

Preparation begins with knowing what you're preparing for. Alvin York knew he was headed for war, and as a result he assessed his personal state of preparation. Likewise, you need to determine where you and your team are headed. You need to examine what the conditions will be along the way. And you need to determine what price you will have to pay to get there. If you don't, you will be unable to prepare yourself properly.

2. Alignment

I enjoy playing golf, and it has taught me a valuable lesson. Although you know where you want to go, you'll never get to your desired destination if you're not lined up right. That's true of personal preparation as well as golf. Good alignment makes success possible. Bad alignment makes success impossible—no matter how much you prepare. You can't just work hard. You have to do the right work.

3. Attitude

Lazy people rarely prepare. Diligent people do, but they sometimes overlook an area that can trip them up when they meet a challenge: they neglect their attitude. To succeed in any endeavor,

> **Courage has no greater ally than preparation, and fear has no greater enemy.**

you must do your homework to take care of the mental aspects of your game. You must prepare physically. But you also must have a positive attitude about yourself, your teammates, and your situation. If you believe in yourself and your teammates, then you set yourself up for success.

4. Action

Ultimately you have to take action. Being prepared means being ready to take that first step when the time comes. Remember this: courage has no greater ally than preparation, and fear has no greater enemy.

REFLECTING ON IT

Are you used to winging it? Do you try to fake it till you make it? Or is solid preparation part of your regular routine? If you continually let your teammates down, you're probably playing in the wrong position or not spending enough time and energy preparing to meet challenges.

BRINGING IT HOME

To improve your preparedness . . .

- *Become a process thinker.* Henry Ford observed, "Before everything else, getting ready is the secret of success." Getting ready requires thinking ahead so that you recognize now what you will need later. Create a system or list for yourself that will help you mentally walk through any process ahead of time, breaking tasks down into steps.

> **Before everything else, getting ready is the secret of success.**
> **—HENRY FORD**

Then determine what preparation will be required to complete each step.

- *Do more research.* People in just about every profession utilize some kind of research to improve themselves. Become more familiar with the research tools of your trade and make yourself an expert at using them.

- *Learn from your mistakes.* The greatest preparation tool can often be a person's own experience. Think about the mistakes you recently made while completing a project or executing a challenge. Write them down, study them, and determine what you can do differently the next time you face a similar situation.

DAILY TAKE-AWAY

In 1946, entertainer Ray Charles heard that Lucky Millinder's band was coming to town. Charles managed to arrange an audition, and that excited him. If he could get on with Millinder, he would be in the big time.

When his opportunity came, the young musician played the piano and sang his heart out. Being blind, Charles couldn't see Millinder's reaction to his performance, so when he was finished, Charles waited patiently for his response. Finally he heard the band leader say, "Ain't good enough, kid." Charles went back to his room and cried.

"That was the best thing that ever happened to me," Charles later recalled. "After I got over feeling sorry for myself, I went back and started practicing so nobody would ever say that to me again." No one has. As the saying goes, "You can claim to be surprised once; after that, you're unprepared." Charles's preparation has paid him dividends for more than half a century, and he has played with some of the most talented musicians in the world. Preparation may not guarantee a win, but it sure puts you in position for one.

> You can claim to be surprised once; after that, you're unprepared.

COMPANION ONLINE RESOURCE

Learn more about yourself and this quality of a team player by taking the FREE assessment at **QualitiesOfATeamPlayer.com**.

13

RELATIONAL

IF YOU GET ALONG, OTHERS WILL GO ALONG

Relationships help us to define who we are and what we can become. Most of us can trace our successes to pivotal relationships.

—Donald O. Clifton and Paula Nelson

Anyone who loves his opinions more than his teammates will advance his opinions but set back his team.

—John C. Maxwell

CONNECTING WITH PEOPLE
WHEREVER THEY ARE

In the early 1960s, Michael Deaver was a young man with a political bent looking for a leader he could believe in and follow. The
person he found was an actor-turned-politician named Ronald
Reagan. In 1966, Reagan was elected governor of California, an
office he would hold for two terms, from 1967 to 1975. During
that tenure, Deaver became Reagan's deputy chief of staff, an office
he also held when Reagan became the nation's fortieth president.

Deaver admired many things about the man he worked with
for thirty years. Ronald Reagan had a lot of remarkable qualities: his convictions and love of country, his understanding of
himself, his skill as a communicator, and his honesty. Deaver
said, "I would go so far as to say that he was actually incapable
of dishonesty."[1] But perhaps what was most impressive about
Ronald Reagan was his ability to relate to people.

Deaver commented, "Ronald Reagan was one of the shyest
men I'd ever met."[2] Yet the president was able to connect with
anyone, whether a head of state, a blue-collar worker, or a feisty
member of the press. When asked about why Reagan had such
rapport with the press corps, Deaver remarked, "Well, Reagan
basically liked people, whether they were part of the press corps
or whether they were just ordinary people. That comes through.
While many of the press wouldn't agree with Reagan's policy,
they genuinely liked him as a person."[3]

Part of Reagan's skill came from his natural charisma and glib verbal aptitude developed in Hollywood. But even greater was his ability to relate to people, something he honed while traveling the country for a decade as the spokesman for General Electric.

It's said that Reagan could make anyone feel like his best friend, even someone he'd never met before. But more important, he connected with the people closest to him. He truly cared about the people on his team. "The chief of staff, or the gardener, or a secretary would all be treated the same, as far as he was concerned," remembered Deaver. "They were all important."[4]

Deaver related a story that tells much about the connection the two men experienced. In 1975, Reagan gave a speech to a group of conservation-minded hunters in San Francisco, and the organization gave him a small bronze lion as a gift. At the time, Deaver admired it and told Governor Reagan how beautiful he thought it was.

Ten years later, Deaver prepared to bring his service to President Reagan to an end after having written his letter of resignation. Reagan asked Deaver to come to the Oval Office the next morning. As the deputy chief of staff entered the room, the president stood in front of his desk to greet him.

"Mike," he said, "all night I've been trying to think of something to give you that would be a reminder of all the great times we had together." Then Reagan turned around and picked up something from his desk. "You kinda liked this little thing, as I recall," the president said, his eyes moist. And he handed the bronze lion to Deaver, who was totally overcome. He couldn't believe that Reagan had remembered that about him all those years. That lion has held a place of honor in Deaver's home ever since.

FLESHING IT OUT

Teams want people who are relational. Everyone liked being around Ronald Reagan because he loved people and connected with them. He understood that relationships are the glue that holds team members together—the more solid the relationships, the more cohesive the team.

> **Relationships are the glue that holds team members together.**

Here is how you know whether you have built solid relationships with other team members. Look for the following five characteristics in your team relationships:

1. Respect

When it comes to relationships, everything begins with respect, with the desire to place value on other people. Human relations author Les Giblin said, "You can't make the other fellow feel important in your presence if you secretly feel that he is a nobody."

The funny thing about respect is that you should show it to others, even before they have done anything to warrant it, simply because they are human beings. But at the same time, you should always expect to have to earn it from others. And the place you earn it the quickest is on difficult ground.

2. Shared Experiences

Respect can lay the foundation for a good relationship, but it alone is not enough. You can't be relational with someone you don't know. It requires shared experiences among teammates over time. And that's not always easy to achieve. For example, when Brian Billick, coach of the

> You can't make the other fellow feel important in your presence if you secretly feel that he is a nobody.
> —LES GIBLIN

2001 Super Bowl Champion Baltimore Ravens, was asked about a team's chances for repeating a championship season, he commented that it would be very difficult. Why? Because 25 to 30 percent of the team changes every year. Newer players don't have the shared experiences with the team that are needed to succeed.

3. Trust

When you respect people and you spend enough time with them to develop shared experiences, you are in a position to develop trust. As I mentioned in regard to the Law of Solid Ground in *The 21 Irrefutable Laws of Leadership*, trust is the foundation of leadership. It is also essential to all good relationships. Scottish poet George Macdonald observed, "To be trusted is a greater compliment than to be loved." Without trust, you cannot sustain any kind of relationship.

4. Reciprocity

One-sided personal relationships don't last. If one person is always the giver and the other is always the receiver, then the relationship will eventually disintegrate. The same is true of relationships on a team. For a team to build and improve relationally, there has to be give-and-take so that everyone benefits as well as gives.

> To be trusted is a greater compliment than to be loved.
>
> —GEORGE MACDONALD

5. Mutual Enjoyment

When relationships grow and start to get solid, the people involved begin to enjoy each other. Just being together can turn even unpleasant tasks into positive experiences. For example, I'm not the kind of person who enjoys running errands or waiting in lines. But sometimes when my wife, Margaret, is planning to run out and tackle her to-do list, I'll go with her simply because I want to be with her. She is my number one teammate, and there's no one in the world I'd rather spend time with. We both benefit. She completes her list, and I'm able to spend time with her.

REFLECTING ON IT

How are you doing when it comes to being relational? Do you spend a lot of time and energy building solid relationships with your teammates, or are you so focused on results that you tend to overlook (or overrun) others as you work to achieve team goals? If the latter is true of you, think about the wise words of George Kienzle and Edward Dare in *Climbing the Executive Ladder:* "Few things will pay you bigger dividends than the time and trouble you take to understand people. Almost nothing will add more to your stature as an executive and a person. Nothing will give you greater satisfaction or bring you more happiness." Becoming a highly relational person brings individual and team success.

B R I N G I N G   I T   H O M E

To better relate to your teammates . . .

- *Focus on others instead of yourself.* The first and most important step in becoming good at relationship building is to start focusing on others rather than yourself. Think about your teammates. How can you add value to them? What can you give them without benefiting yourself? Don't forget that the team is not about you.

- *Ask the right questions.* If you aren't sure about your teammates' hopes, desires, and goals, then you need to ask them. What makes them smile? What makes them cry? What do they dream about? Get to know who they really are by asking the right questions and listening carefully to their answers.

- *Share common experiences.* You will never develop common ground with your teammates unless you share common experiences. Time together while working as a team is essential, but so is spending time together outside that setting. Work to make connections with teammates. Do things socially. Spend time with the families. Find ways to share your lives.

> You will never develop common ground with your teammates unless you share common experiences.

- *Make others feel special.* One of Ronald Reagan's strengths was making everyone on his team feel special. You can do the same thing by giving others your full attention when you're with them, giving them genuine compliments, and recognizing others in front of their peers and family members. People will connect with you when you show them you care about them.

DAILY TAKE-AWAY

Frederick William I, the king of Prussia, was not known for having a pleasant disposition. His passion was his army, and he spent much of his life building it. He had little love for anything or anyone else, including his family. He was often cruel to his son, who eventually succeeded him on the throne as Frederick II, the Great.

The elder Frederick often walked the streets of Berlin alone, and his subjects fled from him. It is said that on one of his walks, a citizen saw him coming and attempted to escape the monarch by ducking into a doorway.

"You," called out the king, "where are you going?"

"Into the house, Your Majesty," replied the nervous man.

"Is it your house?" Frederick pressed.

"No, Your Majesty."

"Then why are you entering it?" the king demanded.

"Well, Your Majesty," the man admitted, worried that he might be thought a burglar, "to avoid you."

"Why?" demanded Frederick.

"Because I fear you, Your Majesty."

Frederick raised his walking stick threateningly at the man and shouted, "You're not supposed to fear me, you scum. You're supposed to love me!"

Teammates seldom go along with someone they can't get along with.

COMPANION ONLINE RESOURCE

Learn more about yourself and this quality of a team player by taking the FREE assessment at **QualitiesOfATeamPlayer.com**.

14

SELF-IMPROVING

TO IMPROVE THE TEAM, IMPROVE YOURSELF

Perfection is what you're striving for,
but perfection is an impossibility.
However, *striving* for perfection is not an impossibility.
Do the best you can under the conditions that exist.
That is what counts.

—*John Wooden*

Learn as if you were to live forever;
live as if you were to die tomorrow.

—*Anonymous*

FROM TREES TO TELEPHONES

If you own or have quick access to a cellular phone, put down this book for a moment and grab the phone. As I am writing this, I've also stopped to get mine. Now look at the manufacturer's name imprinted on the phone. If you're like me—and like nearly one-third of the people in the world who own a cellular phone—then the name on your phone is Nokia.

Knowing that Nokia is the largest producer of cellular phones in the world, you'd probably never guess how the company got its start. It was formed more than a century ago by Fredrik Idestram. In the mid-1860s, as the lumber industry in Finland started to boom, Idestram built a small pulp mill on the Emäkoski River and began making paper. (So I guess you could say that the company has always been in the communication business.)

The first couple of years, the company struggled, especially in Finland. But when Idestram won a bronze medal for his ground-wood pulp at the 1867 Paris World's Fair, Nokia's sales took off, and it soon became firmly established. It excelled not only in its native Finland but explored and established markets in Denmark, Russia, Germany, England, and France. Before long the company had added two more paper facilities.

In the late 1890s, Nokia sought to diversify. The company built a water-driven electric power station near its first mill, and it attracted the Finnish Rubber Works as a customer. After a few years, the rubber company moved its operation to be near Nokia's power plant. Eventually the two companies became partners.

The companies did well during and after World War I. In 1922, they bought a controlling share of the Finnish Cable Works and did even better. They continued selling their existing products from the forestry and rubber industries, but the company's growth for the next forty years was driven by the sales that came from the cable works—items such as power cables, telephone lines, and telephone equipment. By the 1960s, the company had four major business segments: forestry, rubber, cable, and electronics.

During the next two decades, Nokia experienced some difficult times. The one-hundred-year-old company had become a huge conglomerate, and it was losing money. Executives at Nokia knew that the company needed to better its situation.

The solution to Nokia's problems came from an unlikely source. In 1990, a young executive who had been with Nokia for five years was asked to take over the unprofitable mobile-phone division of the company and turn it around. His name was Jorma Ollila, and his background was in finance and banking. He was so successful at the task that he was made the president and CEO of Nokia in 1992.

Ollila's next challenge was to turn the rest of the company around. His strategy was twofold. First, he determined to focus the organization's efforts in the area of greatest potential: communications technology. That meant divesting the company of its other interests, including what had initially launched the company: rubber and paper. Second, Ollila wanted to replace trees with people, meaning that the company recognized that its value lay in human resources, not natural resources. That was especially important for a company whose business is technology. "The key challenge of technology companies today is how we renew ourselves," observes Ollila. "The technology cycles are shorter. We must build on our discontinuities and turn them into our favor."[1]

Ollila personally knows the value of renewing himself. He has earned three master's degrees—in political science, economics, and engineering. He has taken the personal goal of self-improvement and made it a corporate one. The "Nokia Way" is grounded in four objectives: customer satisfaction, respect for the individual, achievement, and continuous learning.

"Continuous learning entitles everybody at Nokia to develop themselves and find ways to improve their performance," says Ollila. "And what's true for the individual is just as true for the company as a whole."[2] To improve a team—even a team of more than sixty thousand people like Nokia—improve the individuals on that team.

That strategy has been right on. Ollila has turned a money-losing conglomerate into a $20 billion global telecommunications enterprise. And Nokia continues to be an innovative leader in its field. Since 1992, the company has introduced fifteen significant market firsts. If your cell phone has a faceplate with a special color or team logo, or it allows you to set it to ring using a fun tune, or it possesses a short-message chat function, you can thank Nokia. The company brought all those ideas to market. And it is still breaking new ground. Why? Because the people on the Nokia team are self-improving, and as long as they keep getting better, so does Nokia.

"I don't think there is any other company which is better placed than we are to tackle the next paradigm," asserts Ollila. "This is an organization where, if you want to prove yourself, if you want to develop yourself, and grow yourself, we will give you the platform."[3]

FLESHING IT OUT

We live in a society with destination disease. Too many people want to do enough to "arrive," and then they want to retire. My friend Kevin Myers says it this way: "Everyone is looking for a quick fix, but what they really need is fitness. People who look for fixes stop doing what's right when pressure is relieved. People who pursue fitness do what they should no matter what the circumstances are." That's what the people at Nokia do. They go after professional fitness, and as a result they are self-improving.

People who are constantly improving themselves make three processes an ongoing cycle in their lives:

1. Preparation

> It's not what you are going to do, but it's what you are doing now that counts.
>
> —NAPOLEON HILL

Napoleon Hill remarked, "It's not what you are going to do, but it's what you are doing now that counts." Self-improving team players think about how they can improve today—not some far-off time in the future. When they get up in the morning, they ask themselves, *What are my potential learning moments today?* Then they try to seize those moments. At the end of the day, they ask themselves, *What have I learned today that I need to learn more about tomorrow?* That positions them to continue growing on an ongoing basis. When individuals are intentional about learning something every day, they become better prepared to handle whatever challenges they meet.

2. Contemplation

I recently came across the following statement: "If you study the lives of the truly great individuals who have influenced the world, you will find that in virtually every case, they spent considerable amounts of time alone—contemplating, meditating, listening."[4] Time alone is essential to self-improvement. It allows you to gain perspective on your failures and successes so that you can learn from them. It gives you the time and space to sharpen your personal or organizational vision. And it enables you to plan how you can improve in the future. If you want to keep getting better, carve out some time to get away and slow down.

> **A time comes when you need to stop waiting for the man you want to become and start being the man you want to be.**
>
> **—BRUCE SPRINGSTEEN**

3. Application

Musician Bruce Springsteen offered this insight: "A time comes when you need to stop waiting for the man you want to become and start being the man you want to be." In other words, you need to apply what you've learned. That is sometimes difficult because it requires change. Most people change only when one of three things happens: they hurt enough that they have to, they learn enough that they want to, or they receive enough that they are able to. Your goal is to keep learning so that you want to change for the better every day.

REFLECTING ON IT

There is nothing noble in being superior to someone else; progress is becoming superior to your previous self. Is that something you strive for? Do you try to become better than you were last year, last month, or last week? Do you look for a way to learn something every day? Or are you hoping to arrive someplace where you no longer have to improve? (Perhaps you believe you've reached that place already.) You can't wait for circumstances or some other person to improve you. You must take responsibility for that yourself. George Knox was right: "When you cease to be better, you cease to be good."

BRINGING IT HOME

To become self-improving . . .

- *Become highly teachable.* Pride is a serious enemy of self-improvement. For a month, put yourself in learning roles whenever possible. Instead of talking in meetings when people ask for advice, listen. Tackle a new discipline, even if it makes you feel inadequate. And ask questions anytime you don't understand something. Adopt the attitude of a learner, not an expert.

> **Pride is a serious enemy of self-improvement.**

- *Plan your progress.* Determine how you will learn on two levels. First, pick an area where you want to improve. Plan what books you will read, conferences you will attend, and experts you will interview for the next six months. Second, find learning moments wherever you can every day so that not a day passes without your experiencing improvement of some kind.

- *Value self-improvement above self-promotion.* King Solomon of ancient Israel said, "Let instruction and knowledge mean more to you than silver or the finest gold. Wisdom is worth much more than precious jewels or anything else you desire."[5] Make your next career move based on how it will improve you personally rather than how it will enhance you financially.

DAILY TAKE-AWAY

In *The 17 Indisputable Laws of Teamwork,* I wrote about pioneer aviator Charles Lindbergh, mentioning that even his solo flight across the Atlantic Ocean was really a team effort, since he had the backing of nine businessmen from St. Louis and the help of the Ryan Aeronautical Company, which built his plane. But that doesn't take away from his personal effort. For more than thirty-three hours, he flew alone and covered an incredible 3,600 miles.

That's not the kind of task a person just goes out and does. He has to work up to it. How did Lindbergh do that? A story from his friend Frank Samuels gives insight into the process. In the 1920s, Lindbergh used to fly mail out of St. Louis. Occasionally he would go out to San Diego to check on the progress of his plane, the *Spirit of St. Louis*, which was being built there. Samuels sometimes went along with him, and the two men would stay overnight in a small hotel there. One night Samuels woke up shortly after midnight and noticed that Lindbergh was sitting by the window looking at the stars. It had been a long day, so Samuels asked, "Why are you sitting there at this hour?"

"Just practicing," answered Lindbergh.

"Practicing what?" asked Samuels.

"Staying awake all night."

When he could have been enjoying a well-deserved rest, Lindbergh was putting forth the effort to improve himself. It's an investment that paid off for him—and it can do the same thing for you.

COMPANION ONLINE RESOURCE

Learn more about yourself and this quality of a team player by taking the FREE assessment at **QualitiesOfATeamPlayer.com**.

15

SELFLESS

THERE IS NO *I* IN TEAM

Life should not be estimated exclusively by the standard of dollars and cents. I am not disposed to complain that I have planted and others have gathered the fruits. A man has cause for regret only when he sows and no one reaps.

—*Charles Goodyear*

When you stop giving and offering something to the rest of the world, it's time to turn out the lights.

—*George Burns*

THE   REAL   MAN   BEHIND   THE   BRIDGE

When the situation is life or death, most people worry more about taking care of themselves than anyone else. Not Philip Toosey. As an officer in the British army during World War II, he had plenty of opportunities to preserve himself, but instead, he always looked out for his team.

In 1927, when the twenty-three-year-old Toosey joined the Territorial Army, a kind of army reserve, he did so because he wanted to do more than merely develop in his career in banking and commodities trading. He had other interests. He was a good athlete and enjoyed playing rugby, but many of his friends were applying for service, so he decided to join as well. He was commissioned as a second lieutenant in an artillery unit where he excelled as a leader and battery commander. In time, he moved up in rank to major.

In 1939, he and his unit were called up to active service as war broke out in Europe. He briefly served in France, was evacuated at Dunkirk, and was subsequently shipped overseas to serve in the Pacific. There he was part of the failed attempt to defend the Malay Peninsula and then finally Singapore from Japanese aggression. By that time, Toosey had been promoted to lieutenant colonel and was in command of the 135th regiment of the army's Eighteenth Division. And although he and his men fought well during the campaign, British forces were repeatedly required to retreat until they fell all the way back to Singapore.

It was there that Toosey displayed the first of many characteristically unselfish acts. When the British realized that surrender was inevitable, Toosey was ordered to leave his men and ship out so that his expertise as an artillery officer might be preserved and used elsewhere. He refused. He later recalled,

> I could not really believe my ears but being a Territorial [rather than a regular army officer] I refused. I got a tremendous rocket and was told to do as I was told. However I was able to say that as a Territorial all orders were a subject of discussion. I pointed out that as a Gunner I had read the Manual of Artillery Training, Volume II, which says quite clearly that in any withdrawal the Commanding Officer leaves last.[1]

He knew the negative effect that abandoning his men would have on their morale, so he stayed with them. Accordingly, when the Allied forces in Singapore surrendered to the Japanese in February 1942, Toosey became a prisoner of war along with his men.

Toosey soon found himself in a POW camp at Tamarkan near a major river called the Kwae Yai. As senior officer, he was in command of the Allied prisoners. His assignment from the Japanese was to build first wooden and then steel and concrete bridges across the river. (The novel and movie *The Bridge on the River Kwai* were based on the events that occurred at this camp, but Toosey was nothing like the character Colonel Nicholson in the movie.)

When first confronted by the orders of his Japanese captors, Toosey wanted to refuse. After all, the Hague Convention of 1907, which the Japanese had ratified, prohibited prisoners of war from being forced to do work that would help their enemies in the war effort. But Toosey also knew that refusal would bring reprisals, which he described as "immediate, physical, and severe."[2] Biographer Peter N. Davies observed, "Toosey, in fact, quickly realized that he had no real option in this matter and accepted that the vital question was not whether the troops were to perform the tasks laid down, but how many were to die in the process."[3]

Toosey chose to ask the prisoners to cooperate with their captors, but he risked his life daily by standing up for his men and arguing for increased rations, regular working hours, and a day off each week. His diligence paid off, though as he later said, "If you took responsibility as I did, it increased your suffering very considerably."[4] He suffered regular beatings and was made to stand at attention in the sun for twelve hours, yet his persistent badgering caused the Japanese to improve conditions for the Allied prisoners. And remarkably during the ten months that work was being done on the bridges, only nine prisoners died.

Later, as the commander of a POW camp hospital, Toosey was known to do everything possible to aid the welfare of his men, including hiking to meet in person every single group of prisoners who arrived at the camp, even in the dead of night. He worked with the black market in order to obtain medicine, food, and other supplies, even though detection would have meant certain death. He insisted on taking responsibility for an illegal radio if it were to be found by Japanese guards. And when the war ended, Toosey's first concern was to find the men of his regiment. He traveled three hundred miles to be reunited with them and determine that they were safe.

After he returned to England, Toosey took three weeks of vacation and then went back to his prewar work with the merchant bank Barings. He never sought glory for his endeavors during the war, nor did he complain about the movie *The Bridge on the River Kwai*, though he evidently hated it. The only thing in his later life related to the war was his work for the Far East Prisoners of War Federation to help other former POWs. It was another act characteristic of a man who always put his team ahead of himself.

FLESHING IT OUT

Poet W. H. Auden quipped, "We're here on earth to do good for others. What the others are here for, I don't know." No team succeeds unless its players put others on the team ahead of themselves. Being selfless isn't easy, but it is necessary.

As a team member, how do you cultivate an attitude of selflessness? Begin by doing the following:

1. Be Generous

St. Francis of Assisi stated, "All getting separates you from others; all giving unites to others." The heart of selflessness is

> All getting separates you from others; all giving unites to others.
>
> —ST. FRANCIS OF ASSISI

generosity. It not only helps to unite the team, but it also helps to advance the team. If team members are willing to give of themselves generously to the team, then it is being set up to succeed.

2. Avoid Internal Politics

One of the worst forms of selfishness can be seen in people who are playing politics on the team. That usually means posturing or positioning themselves for their own benefit, regardless of how it might damage relationships on the team. But good team players worry about the benefit of their teammates more than themselves. That kind of unselfishness helps teammates and benefits the giver. The remarkable scientist Albert Einstein observed, "A person first starts to live when he can live outside of himself."

3. Display Loyalty

If you show loyalty to the people on your team, they will return loyalty in kind. That was certainly the case for Colonel Toosey. Time and time again, he put himself on the line for his men, and as a result they worked hard, served him well, and completed whatever mission they had been given—even in the most difficult of circumstances. Loyalty fosters unity, and unity breeds team success.

> Loyalty fosters unity, and unity breeds team success.

4. *Value Interdependence Over Independence*

In America, we value independence highly because it is often accompanied by innovation, hard work, and a willingness to stand for what's right. But independence taken too far is a characteristic of selfishness, especially if it begins to harm or hinder others. Seneca asserted, "No man can live happily who regards himself alone, who turns everything to his own advantage. You must live for others if you wish to live for yourself."

R E F L E C T I N G   O N   I T

If you want to be a contributing member of a successful team, you have to put others on the team ahead of yourself. How are you when it comes to taking a backseat to others? If someone else gets credit for work well done, does it bother you? If you get bumped from the "starting lineup" of your team, do you shout, pout, or tough it out? All of these things are characteristics of selfless players.

B R I N G I N G   I T   H O M E

To become more selfless . . .

- *Promote someone other than yourself.* If you are in the habit of talking up your achievements and promoting yourself to others, determine to keep silent about yourself and praise others for two weeks. Find positive things to say about people's actions and qualities, especially to their superiors, family, and close friends.

- *Take a subordinate role.* Most people's natural tendency is to take the best place and to let others fend for themselves. All day today, practice the discipline of serving, letting others go first, or taking a subordinate role. Do it for a week and see how it affects your attitude.

- *Give secretly.* Writer John Bunyan maintained, "You have not lived today successfully unless you've done something for someone who can never repay you." If you give to others on your team without their knowing, they cannot repay you. Try it. Get in the habit of doing it and you may not be able to stop.

> You have not lived today successfully unless you've done something for someone who can never repay you.
>
> —JOHN BUNYAN

DAILY TAKE-AWAY

Every fall here in Atlanta, local fans start to get excited about Georgia Tech football. The Tech team is good today, but in the teens, it was an absolute powerhouse. Back in 1916, the Tech team played a tiny law school called Cumberland University, and Tech players were crushing them.

It's said that near the end of the game, Cumberland quarterback Ed Edwards fumbled the snap from center, and as the huge Tech players came barreling into the backfield, he screamed to his fellow backs, "Pick it up! Pick it up!"

The fullback, tired of being pulverized by an opponent, hollered back at the quarterback, "Pick it up yourself—you dropped it." Needless to say, Tech won the game. The final score was 222 to 0.

COMPANION **ONLINE** RESOURCE

Learn more about yourself and this quality of a team player by taking the FREE assessment at **QualitiesOfATeamPlayer.com.**

16

SOLUTION ORIENTED

MAKE A RESOLUTION TO FIND THE SOLUTION

Always listen to experts. They'll tell you what can't be done and why. Then do it.

—*Robert Heinlein*

Don't find fault; find a remedy.

—*Henry Ford*

H I S   A N S W E R   T O   T R A G E D Y

Few things in life are more tragic or disheartening than losing a child. John Walsh, the host of television's *America's Most Wanted,* understands that. In 1981, he and his wife, Reve, lost their six-year-old son, Adam, when the boy was abducted outside a Florida shopping mall and later found murdered. They were devastated.

People react many different ways to such a tragedy. Some parents become defensive and never trust people again. Others sink into depression. Many react in anger and seek revenge. At first, the Walshes were angry. They wanted the murderer found. But they also wanted to sue the department store from which Adam had been abducted. When he first disappeared, no one at the store would help them find their son, and they later discovered that a security guard who worked there had actually ordered six-year-old Adam out of the store. They were outraged.

But the Walshes soon dropped the suit. Instead of focusing on the past, John Walsh possessed a solution-oriented mind-set that looked to the future. He determined that he would try to do something about the problem of child abduction that was becoming increasingly common across the country. He began working to create a national computer system to aid in the search for missing children. He became an advocate for crime victims and lobbied for legislation. And in 1984, Walsh cofounded the National Center for Missing and Exploited Children (NCMEC), an organization that works to prevent child victimization, assists in crime prevention, and acts as a national clearinghouse for information on missing children.

One of the most important child-safety programs NCMEC has developed is called "Code Adam," which has been implemented in more than thirteen thousand stores across the nation. When a customer reports a missing child, a store-wide alert is announced, and a description of the child is given to designated employees, who then search for the child and monitor the exits. If the child isn't found in ten minutes, employees contact the police.[1]

Over the years, the NCMEC team, which now consists of 125 employees, has assisted in more than 73,000 cases involving children, and the group has helped parents to recover more than 48,000 missing children. NCMEC's work has been instrumental in raising the recovery rate of missing children from 60 percent in the 1980s to 91 percent today.[2]

I don't think anyone would have faulted John Walsh if he had withdrawn from people after the death of his son. But because he was solution oriented, he overcame the difficulty of that event, and he has helped tens of thousands of people by bringing together a team to help children.

FLESHING IT OUT

Most people can see problems. That doesn't require any special ability or talent. As Alfred A. Montapert observed, "The majority see the obstacles; the few see the objectives; history records the successes of the latter, while oblivion is the reward of the former."

Someone who thinks in terms of solutions instead of just problems can be a difference maker. A team filled with people who possess that mind-set can really get things done.

Your personality type, upbringing, and personal history may affect how solution oriented you are naturally. However, *anyone* can become solution oriented. Consider these truths that all solution-seeking people recognize:

1. Problems Are a Matter of Perspective

No matter what anyone may tell you, your problems are not your problem. If you believe that something is a problem, then it is. However, if you believe that something is merely a temporary setback, an interim obstacle, or a solution in the making, then you don't have a problem (because you haven't created it).

Obstacles, setbacks, and failures are simply parts of life. You can't avoid them. But that doesn't mean you have to allow them to become problems. The best thing you can do is to meet them with a solution-oriented mind-set. It's just a matter of attitude.

2. All Problems Are Solvable

Some of the great problem solvers have been inventors. Charles Kettering explained, "When I was research head of General Motors and wanted a problem solved, I'd place a table outside the meeting room with a sign: 'Leave slide rules here.' If I didn't do that, I'd find someone reaching for his slide rule. Then he'd be on his feet saying, 'Boss, you can't do it.'" Kettering's approach paved the way for a career that included his holding more than

140 patents, founding Delco, and being inducted into the National Inventors Hall of Fame. He believed all problems were solvable, and he helped to cultivate that attitude in others. If you want to be solution oriented, then you must be willing to cultivate that attitude in yourself too.

3. Problems Either Stop Us or Stretch Us

Orison Swett Marden, founder of *Success* magazine, held that "obstacles will look large or small to you according to whether you are large or small." Problems either hurt you or help you. Depending on how you approach them, they'll stop you from succeeding or stretch you so that you not only overcome them, but also become a better person in the process. The choice is yours.

> Obstacles will look large or small to you according to whether you are large or small.
>
> —ORISON SWETT MARDEN

REFLECTING ON IT

How do you look at life? Do you see a solution in every challenge or a problem in every circumstance? Do your teammates come to you because you have ideas about how to overcome obstacles, or do they avoid telling you about difficulties because you make things *more* difficult? Who you are determines what you see. When it comes to approaching problems, you really have only four choices: flee them, fight them, forget them, or face them. Which do you usually do?

B R I N G I N G   I T   H O M E

To make yourself a more solution-oriented team player . . .

- *Refuse to give up.* At the same moment that one person wants to say, "I give up," someone else facing the same situation is saying, "What a great opportunity!" Think about an impossible situation you and your teammates have all but given up overcoming. Now determine not to give up until you find a solution.

- *Refocus your thinking.* No problem can withstand the assault of sustained thinking. Set aside dedicated time with key teammates to work on the problem. Make sure it's prime think time, not leftover time when you're tired or distracted.

> **No problem can withstand the assault of sustained thinking.**

- *Rethink your strategy.* Nobel Prize–winning physicist Albert Einstein observed, "The significant problems we face cannot be solved at the same level of thinking we were at when we created them." Get out of the box of your typical thinking. Break a few rules. Brain-storm absurd ideas. Redefine the problem. Do whatever it takes to generate fresh ideas and approaches to the problem.

- *Repeat the process.* If at first you don't succeed in solving the problem, keep at it. If you *do* solve the problem, then repeat the process with another problem. Remember, your goal is to cultivate a solution-oriented attitude that you bring into play all the time.

DAILY TAKE-AWAY

In 1939, Soviet troops entered and annexed the Baltic states, including Latvia. The American vice-consul in the Latvian capital of Riga observed what was happening and was concerned that the Soviet soldiers would loot the supply station of the American Red Cross. He wired the U.S. State Department to request permission to fly the American flag over the Red Cross flag to protect the supplies, but the response from his superiors said, "No precedent exists for such action."

The vice-consul climbed the flagpole and secured the American flag to it. Then he sent a message back to the State Department: "As of this date, I have established precedent."

Solutions are usually in the eye of the beholder.

COMPANION ONLINE RESOURCE

Learn more about yourself and this quality of a team player by taking the FREE assessment at **QualitiesOfATeamPlayer.com**.

17

TENACIOUS

NEVER, NEVER, NEVER QUIT

To see far is one thing; going there is another.

—*Constantin Brancusi*

To finish first, you must finish.

—*Rick Mears*

A N O T H E R   F A B   F O U R ?

In the summer of 2001, my wife, Margaret, and I went to England for ten days with our friends Dan and Patti Reiland, Tim and Pam Elmore, and Andy Steimer. We've been close to the Reilands and Elmores about twenty years, and we've done a lot of traveling together, so we were really looking forward to the trip. And though we haven't known Andy nearly as long, he's become a good friend—and he's been to England so many times that he was acting almost like our unofficial tour guide.

As we prepared for the trip, several of us had specific interests and historic sites we wanted to include. For instance, I wanted to visit all the places related to John Wesley, the renowned evangelist of the eighteenth century. For more than thirty years, I've studied Wesley, read all his writings, and collected his books. So we went to Epworth where he grew up, to Wesley's Chapel in London, and to many of the places where he preached. For Tim, we visited Cambridge and other sites related to apologist, professor, and author C. S. Lewis. Andy had only one mustsee place on his list since he had been to England so many times: Winston Churchill's war rooms.

Three of us wanted to walk in the places where our heroes had walked, to get a glimpse of history and maybe understand the sense of destiny one of these great leaders or thinkers must have experienced. Then there was Dan. Sure, Dan enjoyed sharing our interests. He loves the subject of leadership, he's read C. S. Lewis's works, and he is ordained as a *Wesleyan* pastor. And he had a great time visiting our preferred sites. But the one place he absolutely *had* to see was the crosswalk where the Beatles had been photographed for the *Abbey Road* album. Dan wanted us to get our picture taken walking across the street, just as John, Ringo, Paul, and George had.

Now, I like the Beatles, and I thought it might be fun to visit the site. But to Dan, it was more than a big deal. It was essential. If we didn't make it to Abbey Road, then his trip just wouldn't have been complete. Because of that, every day as we set out from our London hotel on our itinerary, Dan would press us intently: "Now, guys, we're going to make it to Abbey Road, right?"

On the last day, we were scheduled to finally make our Abbey Road trek. Everyone except Margaret got up at six o'clock and piled into two cabs to make the trip across town to the street outside the recording studio where the Beatles recorded their last album. Dan was so excited that I thought he was going to bounce off the walls of the cab.

When we got there, we couldn't believe it. The street was closed! Big construction trucks were everywhere, and orange cones filled the crosswalk. It looked as if we had made the trip for nothing. Because we would be leaving London later that afternoon, we wouldn't get another opportunity for the picture. Dan would have to go home empty-handed.

We decided to get out of the cabs anyway, just to check out the situation. We figured there might be heavy construction occurring on the tiny street. However, we discovered that a huge crane, which was located about a half mile away, was scheduled to come down the street sometime in the afternoon, and that's why the road was closed. That gave me hope that we might succeed after all. None of us wanted Dan to be disappointed, and I always love a challenge. So we went to work.

We struck up a conversation with the workmen who had closed the road. At first, they had no idea what we wanted. Then when they understood why we were there, they folded their arms, stood as solid as the Rock of Gibraltar, and told us it couldn't be done. It was their turf, it was their job, and they were not going to move. However, I did have to laugh when we talked to one worker who was about twenty-five years old. When we said that Dan wanted a photo like the one on the Beatles' album, and that the original had been taken on that very spot, the young man said, "Really? It was here?"

We talked to the guys some more. We joked. We offered to take them all out to lunch. And we told them how far we had come and how much the whole thing meant to Dan. "You can be Dan's heroes," I explained. After a while, I could see they were beginning to soften. Finally a big, burly guy with a thick accent said, "Oh, let's help the Yanks out. What could it hurt?"

The next thing we knew, it was like they were working for us. They began clearing cones and moving trucks. They even let Patti, Dan's wife, climb up onto one of the trucks to take the picture so that it would be from the same angle as the Beatles' original shot. Quickly we lined up: first Tim, then Andy, then me (with my shoes off like Paul McCartney), and finally Dan. It was a moment we won't soon forget, and the photo sits on my desk today to remind me of it.

On that summer day in London, did we succeed because of extraordinary talent? No. Was it because of our timing? Certainly not, since our timing got us into trouble in the first place. Was it power or sheer numbers? No, there were only six of us. We succeeded because we were tenacious. Our desire to get that picture was so strong that success for our little team was almost inevitable.

It's appropriate to finish the discussion of the essential qualities of a team player by talking about tenacity because tenacity is crucial to success. Even people who lack talent and fail to cultivate some of the other vital qualities of a team player have a chance to contribute to the team and help it succeed if they possess a tenacious spirit.

Being tenacious means . . .

1. Giving All That You Have, Not More Than You Have

Some people who lack tenacity do so because they mistakenly believe that being tenacious demands from them more than they have to offer. As a result, they don't push themselves. However, being tenacious requires that you give 100 percent—not more, but certainly not less. If you give your all, you afford yourself every opportunity possible for success.

Look at the case of General George Washington. During the entire course of the Revolutionary War, he won only three battles. But he gave all he had, and when he did win, it counted. British general Cornwallis, who surrendered to Washington at Yorktown to end the war, said to the American commander, "Sir, I salute you not only as a great leader of men, but as an indomitable Christian gentleman who wouldn't give up."

2. Working with Determination, Not Waiting on Destiny

Tenacious people don't rely on luck, fate, or destiny for their success. And when conditions become difficult, they keep working.

> ... trying times are
> no time to quit trying.

They know that trying times are no time to quit trying. And that's what makes the difference. For the thousands of people who give up, there is always someone like Thomas Edison, who remarked, "I start where the last man left off."

3. Quitting When the Job Is Done, Not When You're Tired

Robert Strauss stated that "success is a little like wrestling a gorilla. You don't quit when you're tired—you quit when the gorilla is tired." If you want your team to succeed, you have to keep pushing beyond what you *think* you can do and find out what you're really capable of. It's not the first but the last step in the relay race, the last shot in the basketball game, the last yard with the football into the end zone that makes the difference, for that is where the game is won. Motivational author Napoleon Hill summed it up: "Every successful person finds that great success lies just beyond the point when they're convinced their idea is not going to work." Tenacity hangs on until the job is finished.

R EFLECTING ON I T

How tenacious are you? When others have given up, do you keep hanging on? If it's the bottom of the ninth inning and there are two outs, have you already lost the game mentally, or are you ready to rally the team to victory? If the team hasn't found a solution to a problem, are you willing to keep plugging away to the very end in order to succeed? If you sometimes give up before the rest of the team does, you may need a strong dose of tenacity.

B RINGING I T H OME

A. L. Williams says, "You beat 50 percent of the people in America by working hard. You beat another 40 percent by being a person of honesty and integrity and standing for something. The last 10 percent is a dogfight in the free enterprise system." To improve your tenacity . . .

> You beat 50 percent of the people in America by working hard. You beat another 40 percent by being a person of honesty and integrity and standing for something. The last 10 percent is a dogfight in the free enterprise system.
>
> —A. L. WILLIAMS

- *Work harder and/or smarter.* If you tend to be a clock-watcher who never works beyond quitting time no matter what, then you need to change your habits. Put in an additional sixty to ninety minutes of work every day by arriving at work thirty to forty-five minutes early and staying an equal amount of time after your normal hours. If you are someone who already puts in an inordinate number of hours, then spend more time planning to make your working hours more efficient.

- *Stand for something.* To succeed, you must act with absolute integrity. However, if you can add to that the power of purpose, you will possess an additional edge. Write on an index card how your day-to-day work relates to your overall purpose. Then review that card daily to keep your emotional fires burning.

- *Make your work a game.* Nothing feeds tenacity like our natural competitive nature. Try to harness that by making your work a game. Find others in your organization who have similar goals and create a friendly competition with them to motivate you and them.

DAILY TAKE-AWAY

People said it couldn't be done—building a railroad from sea level on the coast of the Pacific Ocean into the Andes Mountains, the second-highest mountain range on earth after the Himalayans. Yet that is what Ernest Malinowski, a Polish-born engineer, wanted to do. In 1859, he proposed building a rail line from Callao on the coast of Peru into the country's interior—to an elevation of more than fifteen thousand feet. If he was successful, it would be the highest railway in the world.

The Andes are treacherous mountains. The altitude makes work difficult, but add to that frigid conditions, glaciers, and the potential for volcanic activity. And the mountains climb from sea level to tens of thousands of feet in a very short distance. Climbing to high altitude in the jagged mountains would require switchbacks, zigzags, and numerous bridges and tunnels.

But Malinowski and his work crews succeeded. Jans S. Plachta states, "There are approximately 100 tunnels and bridges, some of which are major engineering feats. It is difficult to visualize how this task could have been accomplished with relatively primitive construction equipment, high altitudes, and mountainous terrain as obstacles." The railroad still stands today as a testament to the tenacity of the men who built it. No matter what happened to them during the process, Malinowski and his team never, never, never quit.

COMPANION ONLINE RESOURCE

Learn more about yourself and this quality of a team player by taking the FREE assessment at **QualitiesOfATeamPlayer.com**.

CONCLUSION

I hope you have enjoyed *The 17 Essential Qualities of a Team Player* and have benefited from doing the exercises in the "Bringing It Home" section of each chapter. The assignments are designed to help you get a handle on each quality and start the process of continuous personal growth in your life.

I want to encourage you to keep growing as a team member. Review this book periodically to measure how you're developing. Visit the Web site **www.QualitiesOfATeamPlayer.com** to take the free teamwork assessment and put yourself on a regular program of development. If you're looking for resources to help you with that process, contact my organization:

> The INJOY Group
> P.O. Box 7700
> Atlanta, GA 30357-0700
> 800-333-6506

We'll be glad to send you a catalog and current conference schedule.

Keep growing, keep building your team, and never forget, one is too small a number to achieve greatness! Good luck on your journey.

Notes

CHAPTER 1
1. "Perfect Pitch," *Context*, April-May 2001 <www.contextmag.com>.
2. Ibid.
3. Ibid.

CHAPTER 2
1. Rob Davis, "The Real Escape—The Tunnels: 'Tom,' 'Dick' and 'Harry,'" 16 July 2001 <www.historyinfilm.com/escape>.
2. "The Great Escape," 2 July 2001 <www.historyinfilm.com/escape>.
3. Proverbs 27:17.

CHAPTER 3
1. "Jonas Salk, M.D.: Interview, May 16, 1991," 2 July 2001 <www.achievement.org>.
2. Ibid.
3. Frederic Flach, *Choices: Coping Creatively with Personnel Change* (Philadelphia, PA: J. B. Lippincott), 1977.

CHAPTER 4
1. "An Interview with Legendary Coach Herman Boone," 5 January 2001 <www.blackathlete.com>.
2. "Herman Boone, Coach," 29 May 2001 <www.71originaltitans.com>.

3. "Interview with Herman Boone and Bill Yoast," *Remember the Titans* (DVD), Walt Disney Pictures, 2000.

CHAPTER 5
1. Minét Taylor, "Minétspeak," *Wood & Steel*, summer 2001, 3, 5.
2. "From the Beginning," 18 July 2001 <www.taylorguitars.com/history>.
3. "Heartline," December 1993.

CHAPTER 6
1. "Biography," Christopher Reeve home page, 30 July 2001 <www.fortunecity.com>.
2. "New Hopes, New Dreams," *Time*, 26 August 1996 <www.time.com>.
3. Ibid.
4. Ibid.
5. Ibid.

CHAPTER 7
1. Christopher Hosford, "30 Years of Progress for the Ultimate 10-Event Man," *Life Extension* magazine, September 1998, 11 June 2001 <www.lef.org/magazine>.
2. Gordon MacDonald, *The Life God Blesses* (Nashville: Thomas Nelson, 1994).

CHAPTER 8
1. "Edwardian Conquest," 14 June 2001 <www.britannia.com/wales>.

CHAPTER 9
1. "History," 7 August 2001 <www.harley-davidson.com>.
2. Rich Teerlink and Lee Ozley, *More Than a Motorcycle: The Leadership Journey at Harley-Davidson* (Boston: Harvard Business School Press, 2000), 8.

3. "Motorcycle and Customer Data," 7 August 2001 <www.investor. harley-davidson.com>.

4. John C. Maxwell, *Failing Forward: Turning Mistakes into Stepping Stones for Success* (Nashville: Thomas Nelson, 2000), 40–42.

5. "Smell the Roses: Parade Floats in the Making," 28 December 1997 <www.channel2000.com>.

CHAPTER 10

1. Pleasant T. Rowland, "Welcome to Pleasant Company," 26 June 2001 <www.americangirl.com>.

2. "Company Profile," 26 June 2001 <www.americangirl.com>.

CHAPTER 11

1. "Who Was Molly Pitcher?" Garry Stone, 3 August 2001 <uweb. superlink.net/monmouth/molly>.

CHAPTER 12

1. John Perry, *Sgt. York: His Life, Legend, and Legacy* (Nashville: Broadman and Holman, 1997), 97.

2. "Alvin Cullum York," 2 July 2001 <volweb.utk.edu.schools/york>.

3. Gladys Williams, "Alvin C. York," 2 July 2001 <volweb.utk.edu/ schools>.

4. Perry, *Sgt. York*, 32.

5. Williams, "Alvin C. York."

CHAPTER 13

1. Michael K. Deaver, "The Ronald Reagan I Knew," *Parade*, 22 April 2001, 12.

2. Ibid., 10.

3. "Thirty Years with Reagan: A Chat with Author, Former Reagan Aide Michael Deaver," 20 April 2001 <www.abcnews.com>.

4. Ibid.

CHAPTER 14

1. Joyce Routson, "Nokia CEO Talks About Next-Generation Mobile Technology," 6 March 2001 <www.gsb.stanford.edu/news>.
2. "The Nokia Way," 29 June 2001 <www.nokia.com>.
3. John S. McClenahen, "CEO of the Year," 30 November 2000 <www.industryweek.com>.
4. Anonymous.
5. Proverbs 8:10–11, author's paraphrase.

CHAPTER 15

1. Peter N. Davies, *The Man Behind the Bridge: Colonel Toosey and the River Kwai* (London: Athlone Press, 1991), 56.
2. Ibid., 107–8.
3. Ibid., 99.
4. "A Tale of Two Rivers," *Electronic Recorder*, March 1998 <www.livgrad.co.uk>.

CHAPTER 16

1. "Code Adam," 29 May 2001 <www.ncmec.org>.
2. "Our Story," 29 May 2001 <www.ncmec.org>.

JOHN C. MAXWELL, known as America's expert on leadership, is the founder of the INJOY Group, an organization dedicated to helping people maximize their personal and leadership potential. Through his seminars, books, and tapes, Dr. Maxwell encourages and motivates more than one million people each year. He has authored more than twenty-four books, including *The 17 Indisputable Laws of Teamwork*, *The 21 Irrefutable Laws of Leadership*, *Becoming a Person of Influence*, *The Success Journey*, *Developing the Leader Within You*, and *Developing the Leaders Around You*.

RELATIONSHIPS
Be a People Person (Victor Books)
Becoming a Person of Influence (Thomas Nelson)
The Power of Influence (Honor Books)
The Power of Partnership in the Church (J. Countryman)
The Treasure of a Friend (J. Countryman)

EQUIPPING
Developing the Leaders Around You (Thomas Nelson)
Partners in Prayer (Thomas Nelson)
The 17 Indisputable Laws of Teamwork (Thomas Nelson)
The Success Journey (Thomas Nelson)
Success One Day at a Time (J. Countryman)

ATTITUDE
Be All You Can Be (Victor Books)
Failing Forward (Thomas Nelson)
The Power of Thinking (Honor Books)
Living at the Next Level (Thomas Nelson)
Think On These Things (Beacon Hill)
The Winning Attitude (Thomas Nelson)
Your Bridge to a Better Future (Thomas Nelson)
The Power of Attitude (Honor Books)

LEADERSHIP
The 21 Indispensable Qualities of a Leader (Thomas Nelson)
The 21 Irrefutable Laws of Leadership (Thomas Nelson)
The 21 Most Powerful Minutes in a Leader's Day (Thomas Nelson)
Developing the Leader Within You (Thomas Nelson)
The Power of Leadership (Honor Books)

How Can You Be A More Successful Team Player?

John C. Maxwell has the resources for you!

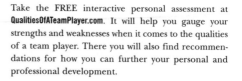

| **STEP 1** | Assess Your Team Player Qualities |

Take the FREE interactive personal assessment at **QualitiesOfATeamPlayer.com**. It will help you gauge your strengths and weaknesses when it comes to the qualities of a team player. There you will also find recommendations for how you can further your personal and professional development.

| **STEP 2** | Start With The Basics |

Spend 17 days reading *The 17 Essential Qualities of A Team Player*. Read one chapter each day to understand the foundations for becoming an invaluable team player.

Leadership expert John C. Maxwell encourages readers to explore and enhance their team player skills. He presents a clear analysis of the personal characteristics necessary for becoming an effective team player.

John's detailed descriptions and many examples are easy to understand and applicable to every area of life.

STEP 3   Invest In Yourself And Your Team

Audio Series

Living the 17 Essential Qualities of a Team Player: Becoming the Kind of Person Every Team Wants
— Audio Application Series

Invest 17 weeks in a personal growth plan that will make you the kind of player every team wants. *Living the 17 Essential Qualities of a Team Player* is an in-depth course, which will supply you with the information and application you need to become more valuable and effective in any team setting.

Video Series

Learning the 17 Indisputable Laws of Teamwork
— Video Application Series

Spend 17 weeks investing in your people by taking them through the *Learning the 17 Indisputable Laws of Teamwork* series. As a team, set aside one hour each week to study one session. The course is designed to teach each person — leaders and followers — how to form productive teams and participate as effective team members.

STEP 4   Continue The Process

Let John C. Maxwell mentor you monthly.

Maximum Impact®
The Monthly Mentoring Leadership Club for Marketplace Leaders
— Audio Program (Available on CD or audiocassette)

Most leaders will agree that regardless of how long they've been in a leadership position, there are issues that they face every day where they would like some insight and helpful perspective. John will provide you with such mentorship on a monthly basis.
Visit **www.INJOY.com/MaxwellMentoring**.

For More Information or to Order...
Visit MaximumImpact.com

Priority Code: 17Q